SHORT CUTS

INTRODUCTIONS TO FILM STUDIES

INTERNATIONAL POLITICS AND FILM

SPACE, VISION, POWER

SEAN CARTER & KLAUS DODDS

WALLFLOWER

LONDON and NEW YORK

A Wallflower Press Book
Published by
Columbia University Press
Publishers Since 1893
New York • Chichester, West Sussex
cup.columbia.edu

Cataloging-in-Publication Data is available from the Library of Congress

ISBN 978-0-231-16971-4 (pbk.)
ISBN 978-0-231-85059-9 (e-book)

Book and cover design: Rob Bowden Design
Cover image: *Syriana* (2005). © Warner Bros.

CONTENTS

Acknowledgements   vii

ACKNOWLEDGEMENTS

We would like to thank Yoram Allon, Commissioning Editor at Wallflower Press, for providing us with the opportunity to contribute to the excellent 'Short Cuts' series. We are even more grateful for the extraordinary patience that he has shown throughout the course of the project.

Both of us have benefited from using film to teach Critical Geopolitics at the University of Exeter and Royal Holloway respectively, and we are grateful for the feedback provided by our students over the years. We have also both benefited enormously from supervising PhD students who have conducted work in the broad fields of culture and geopolitics, and from supportive families, who generously allow us to indulge our interests in film and geopolitics.

The book has been greatly improved by the excellent proofreading skills of Philip Kirby and the efficient compilation of the filmography and index by Rachael Squire. Earlier versions of the book were read by Peter Adey, Jason Dittmer and Nick Gill and we are thankful for their helpful comments. Part of the analysis of *No Man's Land* is based on an unpublished draft of a paper by Sean Carter and Derek McCormack. We are immensely grateful to Derek for allowing us to draw on some of this material.

Of course, any flaws in the writing, argument or analysis rest with the authors.

Sean Carter & Klaus Dodds
April 2014

1   FILM AND INTERNATIONAL POLITICS

In *Syriana* (2005), CIA agent Bob Barnes (George Clooney) is sent to the fictional Middle-Eastern state from which the film takes its title. A complex thriller is constructed around the murky world of inter-state relations, corporate greed and the everyday lives of those caught up in the attempts of more powerful agents to exert some kind of control over energy resources. In this sense the film nicely captures much of what we are interested in exploring in this book, for we take 'international politics' to not just refer to the most dramatic instances of inter-state conflict (such as war) but to a much broader and, in many ways, more mundane set of practices which constitute the political world. Moreover, we see these practices as restricted not just to nation-states (though they remain significant international actors) but as extending to a whole range of actors and interests, including, as *Syriana* suggests, a variety of agents and sites such as CIA operatives, migrant workers, energy analysts, lawyers and their families.

Still, at first glance, many might think that the stuffy world of international politics might have little to do with film and other forms of popular culture. When we were both studying political geography and international relations at British universities in the late 1980s and early 1990s, it was filled with sombre accounts of men (in the main) and particular agents, sites and processes such as diplomats, international summits and foreign policy analysis, respectively. Film and other popular media such as television would have been seen as either entertainment and/or mechanisms for representing the unfolding dramas of international politics. In retrospect, this, we would argue, is a rather restricted view of both international politics and popular culture, including film, and one that inadvertently reveals particular disciplinary engagements.

For us popular media (such as film and television), and social media platforms (such as YouTube and Twitter) help to constitute international politics. Even if we restrict our understanding of the latter to a focus on the interaction of nation-states in an international arena, we would argue that the visual is a crucial element in the enactment of 'states' and the 'international arena'. As with film, we might draw attention to a whole series of creative processes ranging from the choreography of world leaders and their press appearances to scouting for filming locations and the assembly of sets. But the visual is also critical to the exercise of geopolitical power as states and their leaderships attempt to frame and demarcate (including hiding from sight) events, sites and processes.

Perhaps we could even claim that international politics is like film in the sense that it has its generic qualities. When President Bush famously announced in May 2003 that US combat operations were complete, he did so standing on an aircraft carrier mimicking the generic conventions of the techno-thriller, and specifically a classic Reagan-era film, *Top Gun* (1985). Having allegedly flown a naval aircraft onto the deck of the aircraft carrier, Bush emerged in flying suit to dramatically present himself as Commander in Chief, and after changing into a sombre suit and tie he announced in a more statesmanlike manner that hostilities were formally ending in Iraq. The aircraft carrier was actually stationed off the Pacific coast at the time but the intent was surely to use the generic conventions of the techno-thriller to create a particular visual aesthetic involving hyper-masculine agents, force projection, technological sophistication and a determination to prevail against enemies. While ridiculed at the time by his critics, the 'event' itself highlighted the role of creativity and visual practices associated with movie making, and as William Gibson (1991) notes, the technological thriller might be seen as a cultural response to anxieties regarding American 'failures' in Vietnam in the 1960s and 1970s.

While this so-called 'Top Gun' moment neatly reminds us how film, geopolitics and war might interact with one another, this books aims to bring the discipline of International Relations (hereafter IR), and the related field of Critical Geopolitics, into closer contact with visual studies in general, and film studies in particular. While there is evidence of scholarly inter-

Cold War geopolitics as the intersection of masculinity, technology and US power (*Top Gun*, 1985)

President George Bush and his 'Top Gun moment' aboard the USS Abraham Lincoln in May 2003

est, it is only comparatively recently that IR scholars have begun to think about this relationship between international politics and popular culture, including film as more than simply mirror-like (for example, for an early study see Gregg 1998; for more theoretically sophisticated work see Light 2001; Weber 2001, 2006; Shapiro 2008). In other words, there was a tendency to think of film acting as simply a representational medium, one that rather imperfectly represented the complex business of war, diplomacy, statecraft, intelligence and the like. Alternatively, a temptation existed to

3

look at something like the *Harry Potter* film series [2001–11] and then seek to discern visual and narrative 'clues' as to what this might tell us about international politics.

The starting position adopted here is to argue that popular media such as film are an *intrinsic* part of contemporary international politics. Over the last decade, a corpus of work has emerged that contends that international politics can be understood in ways that are not exclusively founded on social science methodologies and associated rational actor paradigms (see, for example, Bleiker 1997; Weldes 1999; Sharp 2000; Weber 2005; Bleiker and Hutchinson 2008; Shapiro 2008). Indeed, some of the very best scholarship now emerging in IR and political geography is exploring how art, film, photography and television not only critique and unsettle taken-for-granted assumptions about the state and state-centric cartographies but also helps to constitute those state-centric cartographies (see Shapiro 2008; Danchev 2009). Film does provide a rich resource for thinking critically about the dominant modes of representation and associated ways of knowing and feeling about international politics, but it is also vital to recognise the inter-relationship between the visual medium and international politics.

It can, as the following chapters suggest, also help to re-populate and reclaim the disembodied tendencies within realist and idealist studies of international politics. 'Realism' refers to a body of theory and practice which tends to prioritise analytical attention on the geopolitics of the state within a supposed anarchical international system. 'Idealism', on the other hand, refers to to an intellectual tradition, which explores the conditions and possibilities for states to co-operate with one another in the international arena. Both realism and idealism assume that the international system is composed of states and that in the absence of a unified world government, they are forced to operate in an uncertain and danger-ous global arena. Realism and idealism also tend to be, as a consequence, largely preoccupied in trying to better understand and even predict the behaviour of states and the international system. In both cases, popular culture in any sense has frequently been neglected in favour of focusing on the serious business of understanding governing elites and their strategic behaviour and reasoning.

As Cynthia Weber (2001) notes, many scholars working within a realist IR framework would not even consider popular media such as film and television worthy of consideration. However, in her estimation, film can be used to puncture some of the central 'myths' underlying IR theorising such as international anarchy as a 'cause' of war. She uses a variety of films to bring to the fore how IR theorists depend upon certain narratives and images to sustain particular understandings of states and the international system, rejecting the notion that the state and the international system are pre-given. This notion is perhaps best explained by David Campbell when he notes:

> If we assume that the state has no ontological status apart from the many and varied practices that bring it into being, then the state is an artifact of a continual process of reproduction that performatively constitutes its identity. The inscription of boundaries, the articulation of coherence and the identification of threats to its sense of self can be located in and driven by the official discourses of government. But they can equally be located in and driven by the cultural discourses of the community, and represented in sites as 'unofficial' as art, film and literature. (2003: 57)

Another way to further unsettle some of the dominant modes of enquiry in IR, then, is to consider how international politics is literally grounded in particular places. The border, for example, is one place or set of places where divisions between the national and the international are identified, visualised, normalised and secured. State-sanctioned authorities such as border patrol guards and immigration officials are not the only actors involved in the making and unmaking of the border though. People and commodities play their part in consolidating, legitimating and subverting the border. They contribute to making visible the border, and the enactment of the visual is itself an expression of geopolitical power. While the border might offer the chimera of security, it can also provide a source of anxiety, as fears are expressed about the flow of drugs, terror and ideas imperilling a 'homeland'. The role of 'distant others' can often be crucial in these particular representations of international politics as can the apparent visual imperative to be seen to be doing something to protect the border by fortifying it. The notion of who belongs and who does not belong becomes all the more urgent in 'exceptional times', such as the on-going War on Terror. Even inside the border, some bodies and faces are more visible than others as governments increasingly encourage their citizens to look out for 'suspicious behaviour'. Additionally, the way in which notions of the 'global' connect to particular places is noteworthy – while terms such as 'globalisation' may have an abstract quality, the connection and intensification of social relations have had distinct consequences for individuals and communities.

It is within these three ideas – the performativity of international politics, the spatialisation of political practice, the role of the visual – that we situate our approach to film and international politics. Thus the first key aim of this book is to argue that film is not just useful to students of international politics because it reflects certain 'real-world' truths, but because film plays a part in the very constitution of the political world in the first place – it is *performative*. As Luiza Bialasiewicz *et al.* argue:

> States are made possible by a wide range of discursive practices that include immigration policies, military deployments and strategies, cultural debates about normal social behaviour, political speeches and economic investments. The meanings, identities, social relations and political assemblages that are enacted in these performances combine the ideal and the material. They are either made or represented in the name of a particular state but that state does not pre-exist those performances. (2007: 406–7)

The second key aim is, then, to argue that it is crucial to attend to the problematic of *space*. In this regard our approach can be situated as emerging from a body of work known as Critical Geopolitics. Whilst not necessarily a cohesive or singular entity, Critical Geopolitics is a broadly post-structuralist approach to the study of international politics that seeks to both re-affirm the significance of geography within international relations whilst also avoiding the reduction of 'geography' to a static, unchanging set of features. In other words, critical geopolitics sees the spaces of international politics not as just a 'backdrop' against which real politics is played out, but as implicated in the performative relations that constitute the realm of international affairs.

A third element that we wish to stress is the role of vision within geopolitical accounts of the world: the manner in which some things, some people, some objects are made more visible than others. Critical Geopolitics emerged, in part, as a critique of the imperial school of geopolitics associated with the early twentieth-century writings of figures such as Halford Mackinder, and accompanying conceits that it was possible to comprehend the world in an all-encompassing and disembodied manner. For Mackinder, advances in geographical knowledge at the end of the nineteenth century offered possibilities for imagining global space in new ways, which in turn offered ways of thinking strategically about global political space. In an address to the Royal Geographical Society in London, in 1904, Mackinder claimed: 'For the first time we can *perceive* something of the real proportion of features and events on the stage of the whole world, and may seek a formula which shall express certain aspects of geographical causation in universal history' (1904: 422; emphasis added).

For Mackinder and other writers in the emerging field of geopolitics at that time, *vision*, or the ability to conceive of global space in particular ways, was an important precursor to their ambition of developing theories of global strategy. Mackinder saw this as primarily predicated upon the complete mapping of the known world, but other ways of comprehending spatial relations were of course also emerging in the late nineteenth and early twentieth centuries, not least cinema itself. As John Agnew contends, 'the modern world is defined by the imaginative ability to transcend the spatial limits imposed by everyday life and contemplate the world conceived and grasped as a picture... The geopolitical imagination's most defining feature is the conception of the world as a single, if divided physical-political entity' (1998: 11). Mackinder saw such visualisation practices as unproblematic, as a function of objective, scientific knowledge rather than subjective, embodied perspective. Taking inspiration from the work of Michel Foucault and Edward Said, in particular, Critical Geopolitics sought to problematise the visual perspective of the 'detached, objective expert', claiming instead that such geopolitical imaginations are always positioned, and always take place within relations of power. It is for these reasons that we subtitle this book 'space, vision, power', for it is the ways in which these three concepts work together through the medium of film that is our interest.

Film, Visual Practices and Everyday Life

While many of us may regard the watching of film and associated activities such as visiting the cinema as a form of entertainment, films are always about something (see Light 2001). If we take Michael Billig's reflections on 'banal nationalism' as an initial guide, film and popular culture more generally contribute to the manufacture of the 'world of nations' and the 'world of the everyday' (1995: 6). As Billig claims, nationalism and, by association, notions of *international* politics are reproduced via a continual iterative process ranging from visual images of national flags to the usage of words such as 'we' and 'them' implying a physical and imaginative geography of both the national and international. Ever since the invention of cinema, governments have recognised the power of the moving image to help constitute understandings (and feelings) about the national, the international, and a whole series of imaginative geographies relating to allies and enemies. Here we briefly discuss ways in which film and international politics can be thought of as co-constitutive.

First, distinguishing the national from the international, especially in times of crisis, is often vital in terms of identity formation and morale building. As David Campbell (1998) has shown, via his examination of American security, a whole series of discursive and material practices have been deployed in order to secure ideas and expressions of national citizenship and national identity. In the nineteenth century, for instance, indigenous American Indian populations were frequently depicted as obstacles to the progression of the American frontier. In Michael Shapiro's (1997) terms 'architectures of enmity' have been critical to the making of sovereign states and Japanese-American, African-American and Arab-American communities have all unwittingly been transformed into 'distant others' in order to sustain particular national identity claims. D. W. Griffith's *Birth of a Nation* (1915) is one well-known and controversial example of how a cinematic engagement with pre- and post-Civil War America contributed to national debates about white supremacy, racial integration and the future of the United States. In the post-war period, films such as *The Searchers* (1956) have also attracted interest as particular expressions of Cold War US identity (as a film about the nineteenth-century frontier being 'read' as an allegorical tale of America's global struggle with the Soviet Union and communist ideologies, for example).

Films, along with mass media generally, play their part in reproducing those banal forms of nationalism and internationalism. These representations of the national and international are consumed within everyday contexts. While governmental discourses concerning, for example, immigration and national security are often expressed in highly rationalised terms, film can provide a rich medium for showing how these policy-orientated concerns manifest themselves in everyday life and in so doing evoke feelings of anger, happiness, fear, humiliation and shame. Films, in their more provocative sense, can unsettle taken-for-granted assumptions about international politics and help to remind us how the visual more generally is an intimate part of modern state power.

Second, heads of state have long recognised that film has the capacity to grab the attention of mass audiences. Hitler's Nazi Germany, Stalin's Soviet Union and Mussolini's Italy provide some of the most compelling illustrations of how fascist and communist regimes encouraged film for the purpose of either promoting a sense of national purpose or excoriating others deemed to be threatening and unwelcome. Democratic countries such as Great Britain and the United States also recognise the power of film to influence opinion and to hold the attention of audiences, especially at moments of crisis and dislocation. Perhaps what films do, then, is to reinforce a fundamentally *habitual* form of geopolitics based on invoking and reinforcing those banal expressions of national identity and architectures of enmity.

Governments have been able to mobilise the possibilities offered by film in part because the film industry in many countries has enjoyed a close relationship with various organs of the state. In the case of Hollywood, for example, the major studios have collaborated closely with the military and intelligence agencies such as the CIA to produce films that were and are judged to offer positive impressions of the US armed forces (e.g. *The Longest Day*, 1962). In return for offering access to bases, equipment and personnel, the Department of Defense avails itself of opportunities to review and propose changes to screenplays (see Robb 2004). In the case of the oft-cited *Top Gun*, the US Navy allowed the filmmakers access to naval bases and ships including an aircraft carrier in return for changes to the script such as the decision to cast Kelly McGillis's character 'Charlie' as a civilian (Tom Cruise) (rather than military person) so that her affair with the aviator Maverick would not appear to condone affairs within the US Navy. But more substantively, the film was intended to reinforce a post-Vietnam habitual geopolitics whereby citizens could be assured that the United States could literally show the world that it had the men and machines required to defend itself against its enemies.

Arguably, we have witnessed the consolidation of what James Der Derian (2008) memorably called the military-industrial-media-entertainment complex, which has blurred the distinction between waging, watching and playing war. Video game development, filmmaking and war waging are now thoroughly intertwined with one another – watch *Black Hawk Down* (2001) and then play the video game and watch how governments increasingly seek to engage with international politics in 'game-like' ways – the search for weapons of mass destruction in Iraq in 2003 began to resemble a quest thriller one might associate with the hyper-masculine figure of Dr Indiana Jones (see Power 2007). Most dramatically, in November 2001, top Hollywood executives and Jack Valenti, chairman of the Motion Picture Association of America, met with Bush administration officials in Beverly Hills to discuss ways that the entertainment industry could contribute to the so-called War on Terror. The then-White House strategist Karl Rove attended the meeting and stressed the need for the entertainment industry to help develop a 'narrative' about America's response to 9/11 (see Cooper 2001). As actors Susan Sarandon, Tim Robbins and Sean Penn demonstrated, this apparent 'call to arms' was not uncritically received.

Third, films do not just represent particular events or stories but they also help to create understandings of who we think we are, how we regard other people and countries and the nature of group or societal membership (see Light 2001). To provide one example, we might turn to the Kazakh reaction to the release of *Borat: Cultural Leanings of America for Make Benefit Glorious Nation of Kazakhstan* (2006). Played by the British comic actor, Sacha Baron Cohen, the film portrays the US-based adventures of a Kazakh journalist called Borat Sagdiyev. Although the film was widely interpreted as a comedy, which revealed insights into the nature of post 9/11 America, it also represents Kazakhstan as economically backward, anti-Semitic and anti-Roma. The president of Kazakhstan placed advertisements in the *New York Times* and other major American media denouncing the film and challenging the stereotypes presented within it. At the same time, this oil-rich Central Asian state is also investing in its own film industry, including the release of *Mongol* (2007) which portrays Genghis Khan and his conquest of the Asian steppes. The film, like an earlier one, *Köshpendiler* (*Nomad*, 2005), aims to represent Kazakhstan as the inheritor of Mongol traits such as bravery, fortitude and physical strength rather than, as *Air Force One* (1997) suggested, a place characterised by corruption, terrorism and post-Soviet instability. Both the makers of *Borat* and the President of Kazakhstan appeared mindful of the power of film and visual culture to constitute public understandings and engagements of and with this particular Central Asian republic.

Michael Moore's documentary *Fahrenheit 9/11* (2004) provides another such example. Already well-known for his distinct documentary style, which had previously explored economic restructuring (*Roger and Me*, 1989), US/Canadian relations (*Canadian Bacon*, 1995) and gun culture (*Bowling for Columbine*, 2002), *Fahrenheit 9/11* sought to directly influence the outcome of the 2004 US presidential election given that it was meant to be an exposé of President George W. Bush's personal background, his lacklustre first-term performance and a biting analysis of US/Saudi relations. Although unsuccessful in terms of securing the election of Senator John Kerry in 2004, the film provoked the anger of conservatives within America and provoked tension in the US/Saudi relationship, which Moore depicts as being based on mutual enrichment and turning a 'blind eye' to the funding of Islamic radicalism by members of the Saudi royal family. For supporters of Moore, he was attempting to mobilise the visual to make visible aspects of international politics that the US government wished to obscure and indeed hide.

Fourth, film can expose and provoke reaction to the norms, practices and values that constitute our habitual engagements with international politics. *The Kingdom* (2007) might be a case in point. It is explicitly concerned with the contentious 'right' of FBI agents to track down and eventually kill Islamic militants inside Saudi Arabia in response to a massacre of American citizens living in a gated community in the country. Although the FBI team secure the co-operation of Saudi officials, there is nonetheless an extraordinary projection of power fuelled by a sense of righteousness that the massacre had to be avenged. American ingenuity, bravery and determination are visually foregrounded at the expense of hooded enemy combatants who are barely seen and incapable of negotiation let alone restraint.

Even if critics might complain that films provide fleeting contextual details about a particular episode such as a specific conflict or crisis, they frequently normalise the dominant political architecture of international politics – a world composed of states with their sovereign domains and boundaries. A good example would be the film *Thirteen Days* (2000), which shows how the Cuban Missile Crisis of 1962 unfolded from the perspective of the Kennedy administration and its staff. Whatever the film's shortcomings in terms of historical accuracy, it provides insights into crisis management and the international politics of US/Soviet and US/Cuban relations. The United Nations provides an important filmic and political backdrop for the famous confrontation between the US and Soviet representatives over whether the latter was stationing missiles in Cuba. The film represents the crisis as a political triumph for President Kennedy but at the same time does not offer any critical questioning of the actual nuclear arms race and the kind of grim logic that persuaded both sides to station nuclear missiles so close to their rival's national borders.

While films may frequently reflect such norms, values and practices to be found within the international political arena, they can also challenge, critique (e.g. *Dirty Wars*, 2013) and ridicule (e.g. *In the Loop*, 2009). Another good example is the French film *OSS 117: Le Caire, Nid D'espions* (*OSS 117: Cairo, Nest of Spies*, 2006), which is not only a parody of the spy thriller genre but a withering critique of what Derek Gregory (2004) has labelled the 'colonial present'. Set in Cairo in 1955, a French secret agent, OSS-117, played by Jean Dujardin, is sent to investigate the disappearance of a fellow agent, Jack Jefferson (Phillipe Lefebvre). His boss tells him that Cairo is, 'the land of pharaohs and pyramids and a veritable nest of spies'. Allegedly working undercover managing a chicken factory, OSS-117 blunders around Cairo, while managing to offend even his closest allies either with his dismissive comments about Egypt and the Arabic-speaking world more generally or with his extraordinary cultural ignorance concerning Islam. He is able to secure some kind of cultural and geographical refuge in the French Embassy, where he can toast 'the French Empire' with a colleague, even if they acknowledge 'unrest in Algeria, Morocco, Tunisia, [and] the fall of Dien Bien Phu'. Unbeknown to him, he stumbles across Russians, former Nazis and Arab nationalists eager to pursue their particular agendas. As OSS-117 later discovers, Jack is not dead but actually masterminding an arms deal in Cairo. After a showdown with Jack, OSS-117 blows up the arms shipment and is later congratulated for his excellent work by his superiors back in France – his next mission is to be sent to Iran. As OSS-117 concludes, 'Westerners are appreciated everywhere, if we show goodwill'. While France played no role in the US-led invasion of Iraq in 2003, the film is a timely reminder of longer political but also visual trajectories of Euro-American imperialism in the Middle East (for example, those associated with Orientalism to use Edward Said's famous term) and the implausibility of white Europeans operating as spies in cultures they barely understand let alone empathise with.

In a rather different vein, films can also represent very different worlds that have yet to happen. One common trope, especially in science fiction and futuristic action-thrillers, is to imagine a world that has been devastated by spectacular events such as a nuclear holocaust (e.g. *Elysium* (2013) and *After Earth* (2013)). One popular example from the 1970s and 1980s was the *Mad Max* trilogy (1979, 1981, 1985), which made a star out of Mel Gibson. Filmed in the semi-desert terrain of New South Wales, the setting is in a post-nuclear holocaust world where the normal fabric of society has been dismantled. The first film in particular represents the country as being at the mercy of road warriors who in their desperate search for fuel (and presumably water and food) will stop at nothing to secure their needs. Max, as a police interceptor, is left with the seemingly hopeless task of imposing law and order in a world that realists would understand as anarchical. International relations appear to have no bearing any more because the world is reduced to a few residuals of basic life. The normal order of things has been radically reversed and Max, after the death of his family, is left to find some kind of redemption through violence and revenge in the anarchic world of the roads that criss-cross this unforgiving environment. Max's travails arguably anticipate some of the more dystopian predictions by writers such as Robert Kaplan (1994) concerning the post-Cold War 'coming anarchy', and have also found more contemporary cinematic resonance in the recent film adaptation of Cormac McCarthy's novel *The Road* (2009).

This book thus makes the case that film and international politics can be successfully studied together. Film can provide a rich source of material regarding popular representations of the Cold War or specific moments such as the Vietnam conflict, the 1991 Gulf War, the September 11th 2001 attacks on the United States or the War on Terror. As a popular archive, they also endure and can, as recent events have illustrated, be re-visited. The much-lauded film *La Battaglia di Algeri* (*The Battle of Algiers*, 1966) remains an important visual testimony of French colonial aggression in Algeria during the 1950s. However, it has also been regularly cited more recently as a vehicle for exploring contemporary colonial violence in Iraq.

Issues such as torture (depicted here in *The Battle of Algiers*) can resonant across different historical and geographical contexts.

Numerous commentators have drawn attention to the fact that the film considers how self-defeating torture was when carried out by the French soldiers and that the dehumanisation of the Algerians caused a profound crisis to the ideals of the French Republic. Poignantly, as it turns out, there were reports that the Pentagon was organising private screenings of the film in order to warn US personnel serving in Iraq about the dangers posed by foreign occupation. As with other films such as *The Siege* (1998), *The Battle of Algiers* has been widely regarded as prescient, profound and anything but *mere* entertainment.

Understanding Movies

This short book cannot offer an exhaustive survey of even Hollywood's engagement with topics and themes that might be considered to be of relevance to international politics. Nor can it offer an exhaustive sense of how one might study film. It has, by necessity, had to be selective, both conceptually and empirically. The examples provided here are intended to provoke further thought on how international politics is thoroughly immersed in a variety of visual cultures, including film. If David Campbell is right that the state is not pre-given then what should interest us is how visual practices are essential in conjuring up the state and exercises of geopolitical power, whether it be through summitry, displays, surveillance or diplomacy.

So the filmic examples are mindful of that wider agenda. On our choices for this book we should note that there are certain generic categories that feature more strongly than others, such as the action-thriller as opposed to the romantic comedy. Genre is relevant because it shapes not only narrative and visual structures but also embodied subject positions. The Hollywood action-thriller, for example, often features strong male lead actors (usually white and American with 'strong bodies') and the narrative arc in combination with subject characterisation encourages viewers to identify with their missions/objectives/hopes/fears rather than those of their potential adversaries or even third parties (see *The Hurt Locker* (2008), for example). One egregious example is the film *Taken* (2008), which features a former special operations officer battling against sadistic Albanian mobsters and Middle Eastern paedophiles in an attempt to save his kidnapped daughter from becoming a sex slave. The lead character's violence is justified, visually and narratively, by a desire to save his daughter from sexual violence operating in a world where the existing law and order system of the French government is judged to be inadequate, corrupt and too slow.

Major studios like generic films such as the action-thriller because they can be pre-sold to audiences that can readily anticipate likely narratives and subject positions. Generic movies do vary in popularity over time, and they can problematise those conventions regarding narrative arcs and subject positions. *The Long Kiss Goodnight* (1996) provides one such example of a strong female lead that participates in a complex plot involving past CIA operations, sexual violence, multiple identities and a bomb plot in the Niagara Falls area. One important aspect of the movie is the focus on the everyday life of a single mother working as a schoolteacher as if to emphasise the mundane nature and banality of her existence. However, as the story unfolds it becomes clear that the principal character, Samantha (Geena Davis), might have enjoyed a past life as a professional CIA officer. What makes the film noteworthy is the casting of a single mother as the lead, and the subsequent reflections on how domestic and international life are gendered, and how the security practices of the state are interwoven with everyday life.

The action-thriller is one of the most durable forms of generic film and features strongly in this account precisely because there are powerful 'insights' into how the state, security and the international system are assembled and performed. In post-9/11 America, the action-thriller, espe-

Black Hawk Down and the reclaiming of a heroic narrative from apparent military failure

cially movies associated with what has been termed 'warrior geopolitics' (which involve military action and 'values' such as masculine valour and bravery) were more successful than more explicitly contemporary 'War on Terror movies', depicting torture and extra-judicial killing in Afghanistan and Iraq (see Dalby 2008). Audiences, so the argument goes, watched films such as *Black Hawk Down* (2001) because they wanted to identify through various embodied subject positions that 'America' possessed the kind of men and equipment deemed necessary to deal with the onset of the War on Terror. It also offered a form of visual catharsis – rather than dwell on the failure of the American operation in 1992, attention was directed towards qualities such as bravery, fraternity and leadership. The film's release date (28th December 2001) was brought forward because it was thought to be likely to be particularly popular with audiences at that time, and this proved to be true in the case of the United States (see Carter and McCormack 2006). It was less popular in other countries such as France, Germany and Japan. In Somalia, crowds apparently cheered when they watched the American helicopters being shot down by militia forces within Mogadishu.

Lawrence Wright (2007), in his award-winning account of the events leading up to 9/11, has argued that 'warrior' films such as *Black Hawk Down*, *We Were Soldiers* (2002) and *Tears of the Sun* (2003) are one way of showing the world that the United States has the capacity to engage militarily with enemies and, if necessary, endure losses. These films and others discussed in subsequent chapters are noteworthy because of the manner in which the individual and small groups of Americans either prevail in the face of tremendous odds, or help others survive tribal violence as in the case of *Tears of the Sun*.

It is also worth acknowledging that other types of movies, including the historical/fantasy epic, have been immensely popular, such as the *Lord of the Rings* trilogy (2001, 2002, 2003), *300* (2006) and *300: Rise of an Empire* (2014). As Damon Young (2007) has noted, films such as *300* (which depicts the battle between the Spartans and the Persians at Thermopylae) depend on a melodramatic plotline, which involves villainy, victimisation, retribution and the seminal role of redemptive violence (one might also add that such films, and perhaps *300* in particular, also rely on familiar orientalist tropes that position enemies and mobilise architectures of enmity). It also lionises the male Spartan warriors and their willingness to fight against unbelievable odds in defence of their families and way of life. In both post-9/11 action thrillers and historical fantasies considerable emphasis has been placed on what Jasbir Puar (2006) has termed 'homonormativities' – a privileging of particular ideologies and practices associated with heterosexual manliness, strong and resilient male bodies, and homo-social relations especially within the military. A cycle of super-hero movies, including *The Fantastic Four* (2007), *The Avengers* (2012) and *The Dark Knight Rises* (2012) are also testament to this

In terms of understanding the complex relationship between film and international politics, attention needs to be given to the importance of inter-textual contexts. Whilst the arguments that we develop in this book do not constitute 'audience research', it is nevertheless important to recognise some of the contexts in which audiences consume, engage with and make sense of film. The development of the so-called blockbuster film in the 1970s had implications for development of the audience as a market. With the release of films such as *Jaws* (1975) and *Star Wars* (1977), a new generation of films began to emerge which placed emphasis on fast-paced and spectacular productions. Plot development was modest and the emphasis was on entertainment, which of course can include films that, in a counter-intuitive vein, are still thought-provoking. One of the key reasons for such a development is commercial appeal, which transcends the geographical boundaries of the United States and the English-speaking world. As Trevor McCrisken and Andrew Pepper have noted:

> Their form tells a different story: that is, their reliance on spectacular action sequences, their provision of trite shocks and constant reassurance, and their insistence that audiences succumb to

the easy stimuli and sensation provided by computer-generated images of over-determined historical events robbed of their particular significance, means that they are just as intelligible and also appealing to audiences in Hong Kong as in Houston. (2005: 203)

As we have noted, some films may connect better with audiences because they are seen to be either prescient or simply indicative of a general mood. Timing of course can be crucial here. The film *Collateral Damage* (2002) was unquestionably a 'victim' of bad timing, as its release was intended for September 2001. Even if it was indeed prescient in terms of identifying the spectral presence of terrorism, it was swiftly recognised that American audiences were unlikely to rush to see a film that featured Colombian terrorists bombing government buildings in Washington DC. While Arnold Schwarzenegger added star appeal, even his presence did not prevent the film from having its release delayed and, by his standards, poor box office receipts (see Carter and Dodds 2011 for further discussion on the relative commercial failure of the post-9/11 'War on Terror movie').

Other forms of media, including television, computer games and social networks, provide another inter-textual context, which help shape the ways that audiences understand and engage with film (and indeed politics). In post-9/11 America, it has become increasingly commonplace for films such as *Black Hawk Down* to generate subsequent video game development alongside game developers such as KUMA who offer countless missions in Afghanistan, Iraq and Iran. Action thrillers and science fiction films have proven particularly adept at being marketed by the video game industry in close association with film studios. This can in turn have further implications for the popularity of those films especially when released on DVD. As Marcus Power has noted, 'Games also offer a (cinematic) romanticisation of war that is both seductive and powerful, and they can provide a (heroic) experience [for the player] of winning a war single-handedly' (2007: 286).

Structure of This Study

As we have already outlined, we take an avowedly spatial approach to our analysis of both cinema and international politics. This is made manifest in the four chapters that together form the main part of this book. Each of these chapters takes a different spatial formation as its organising theme – 'Borders', 'Exceptional Spaces', 'Distant Others' and 'Homeland'. Each theme is interrogated through a detailed discussion and analysis of a number of relevant films. A concluding section to each chapter attempts to make more explicit the relation between the films in question and the spatial and cultural politics at work therein. Throughout we seek to bring academic literatures from the fields of political geography and international relations into dialogue with the field of visual culture, in general, and cinema studies, in particular.

Chapter two considers two American films, *The Terminal* (2004) and *Traffic* (2000) and one film from Palestine, *Yadon Ilaheyya* (*Divine Intervention*, 2002). We place these films within a long-standing tradition of 'border films' and suggest that such films are especially useful in highlighting the ways in which borders need to be understood as both material and discursive.

Chapter three discusses three Hollywood films; *The Siege* (1998), *Iron Man* (2008) and *Rendition* (2007). These films are placed into dialogue with the notion of the 'state of exception': a key idea in political thought that has largely emerged in the wake of the War on Terror pursued by the United States and the 'coalition of the willing' in the years since 2001. Understood as the suspension of the law under conditions of emergency, we discuss how the exceptional powers utilised by the US (and others) has given rise to a series of exceptional spaces. Through an analysis of a fourth film, *The Road to Guantánamo* (2006), we further discuss the potential that cinema provides for making these sites visible, and for helping us to understand the ways that such sites are connected to the more mundane spaces of everyday life. Nevertheless, we remain sceptical of the ability of much mainstream cinema to effectively deal with the complex politics of such issues.

Chapter four considers films from a range of cinematic cultures; Nicija Zemlja (*No Man's Land*, 2001) from Bosnia, the American *Tears of the Sun* and *Kurtlar Vadisi – Irak* (*Valley of the Wolves: Iraq*, 2006) from Turkey, and is interested in the ways in which the 'distant other' is represented and made to be 'distant'. Or, to put it another way, how does cinematic representation contribute to wider processes of the construction of moral distance/proximity? Taking the work of Edward Said on Orientalism as a starting point, the argument in the chapter progresses to discuss how questions of humanitarian intervention (or non-intervention) rely upon such discursive constructions of responsibility.

Chapter five discusses the British film (*Dirty Pretty Things* 2002), *Das Leben der Anderen (The Lives of Others,* 2006) from Germany and the Lebanese release *Sous les Bombes (Under the Bombs*, 2007) in exploring how films might help us consider ideas related to notions of the homeland and belonging, and works towards a concluding discussion around the ability of film to intervene in debates on inclusion and exclusion, through a consideration of a fourth, the American film *Three Kings* (1999).

In our final, concluding chapter, we synthesise the arguments that run throughout the book by focusing, firstly, on the agents, processes and sites that constitute the realm where international politics and film collide, secondly, by thinking through the conceptual issues of materiality, film, and politics, and thirdly, by returning to the key themes of space, vision and power.

2   BORDERS

Borders, as John Agnew has reminded us, are integral to the making of the nation-state (2008). The modern nation-state's evolution depends in large part on clearly delineated borders. Various technologies of the state, such as passport and citizenship laws, help to regulate and identify the limits of such states. Borders demarcate notions of the 'national' and 'international' and other distinctions between the 'citizen' and the 'alien'. They also serve as both 'bridges' and 'barriers', which in turn regulate the movement of people, ideas, goods and, as many governments now acknowledge, terrorist networks. The border and accompanying border zones are usually recognisable by the presence of security officers and associated infrastructure; checkpoints, gates and signage expressing territorial ownership, regulatory authority and associated restrictions on movement. It is, then, physical, material and tangible, whilst also being symbolic, discursive, metaphorical and performative. The status of the border can therefore generate expressions of fear and hope – fear of exclusion, and hope that for some it might lead to the prospect of a better and more secure life.

Border politics, therefore, can be considered as the ways in which states and state-sanctioned authorities control (or seek to control) the movement of people and goods through border politics. Indeed, the ability to control one's borders can be seen as one of the key powers of the state; 'Modern nation-states ... rest their strength and legitimacy fundamentally on their capacities to monitor and control the flow of people and resources into and through their bounded territories' (Herbert 2008: 1). This, however, introduces a contradiction into the heart of the capitalist state. On the one hand, capitalism requires the relatively free flow of capital, goods and, to a lesser extent, people. On the other, states seek to police their borders to limit obligations to their citizens alone.

Prior to 9/11 then, for many Western states including the United States, the primary concern was keeping out 'illegal immigrants', justified on the basis of protecting domestic labour markets and the distribution of resources. The need to control the border zone was thus a major element in the domestic political life of European and North American countries throughout the latter half of the twentieth century (more particular, and perhaps peculiar, border issues were also raised in the context of the Cold War, not least in Berlin – see the discussion on *The Lives of Others* in chapter five for more on this). Hollywood films such as *The Border* (1982) and *Flashpoint* (1984) actively reflected the specific concerns of border security between the US and Mexico in Reagan's America. After 9/11, however, this border, and borders more generally, became far more a site for anxiety about terrorists and terror groups and the danger posed to the domestic societies of Western states. Earlier optimism about globalisation sweeping away borders in the 1990s, especially prominent in neo-liberal readings of the global economy (see Ohmae 1999, for example) was hurriedly replaced with a new discourse based on security and the integrity of national territory.

Political geographers make an important distinction between borders and boundaries (see Newman and Paasi 1998). The latter is generally considered to be a strict line of separation between two distinct territories. The border, which is our preferred term, emphasises a space of interaction and gradual separation between two sovereign entities. In this sense, borders are a paradoxical space – being both the line along which two political entities are separated, but also being the zone of connection and crossing between these distinct political entities. The management and regulation of borders thus becomes an important aspect of how states 'see' their populations and territories, as well as how they 'see' the citizens of other states (see Scott 1998). Borders thus become sites of conflict and negotiation. Such conflicts arise over the rules that govern access across borders, the specific practices of enacting these rules, and the attempted subversion of these rules by a range of actors. Put crudely, state-based agencies alongside private organisations, on the one hand, are charged with patrolling and protecting border zones; while, on the other hand, others might seek to subvert and undermine such management through the smuggling of people and commodities, including drugs, weapons and money '(see, for example, *No Country for Old Men* (2007) and *Border Run* (2012)).

This in turn produces unequal geographies of access. People cross borders daily; but for some their spoken language, dress and even appearance may impede and even prevent their progress. For the poorest and most desperate, the border crossing can be a dangerous and furtive affair as detailed in Courtney Hunt's portrayal of illegal immigration, indigenous politics and working-class border life in *Frozen River* (2008). For those attempting to enter the United States from Mexico or Europe from Africa, the desert and sea respectively represent formidable environmental barriers to even be in sight of the border. Even at that point, safety is not assured as the refugee and migrant navigate the perils posed by people smugglers, border patrol staff and even vigilante citizens, especially on the American side of the border. But, as Louise Amoore (2006) has also noted, the border is also increasingly biometric in form. The collection and assessment of biographical data via retinal scans and fingerprinting at checkpoints is becoming increasingly the norm for both citizens and non-citizens alike. This data is then catalogued and distributed to various government and international agencies through shared databases. Information on an individual and their border crossings is a major source of concern in the contemporary era.

Cinema, alongside other forms of media, has played a critical role in sustaining and reproducing what might be termed border narratives and representations (see Mains 2004). In the case of Hollywood, the most notable cinematic border is the US/Mexican border, which has generated a significant number of films. Ranging from *Border Incident* (1949) to *Babel* (2006) and, more recently, *Crossing Over* (2009) and *Monsters* (2010), generic traditions associated with police procedural, film noir and the action-thriller blend and blur with one another as these films confront the unequal geographies and political contexts of the border. What film is able to do, in these aforementioned examples, is to dramatise the everyday displays of sovereign power by the state – to patrol, to regulate, to police and to resist border crossings. As Michael Kearney has noted, 'It is in the border area that identities are assigned and taken, withheld and rejected. The state seeks a monopoly on the power to assign identities to those who enter this space' (1991: 58).

Other cinematic traditions have also produced their own border films. In the case of Israeli and Palestinian filmmakers, for instance, the so-called 'roadblock movie' has considered in a variety of ways from the action-thriller to satirical comedy the role that border-crossings play in shaping everyday life – examples include *Al qods fee yom akhar* (*Rana's Wedding*, 2002), *Paradise Now* (2005) and *Beit-Lehem* (*Bethlehem*, 2013) (see Zanger 2005; Gertz and Khleifi 2007). In South Asia, there is a rich and varied tradition that has considered the enduring legacies of partition and the subsequent conflicts involving East and West Pakistan. The War on Terror has also generated a new series of cinematic engagements which invoke the presence of the border other, including *A Wednesday* (2008) which involves a Mumbai-based storyline containing terrorists trained and financed from Pakistan. The border and the kinds of films that it has inspired are multiple in generic and narrative forms. There is no one 'border film' *per se*.

This chapter considers how film reminds us how the demarcation and management of the border and border politics more generally is enacted through the visual. The border (whatever its form) is never a neutral line of separation. The first theme concerns border management in the confined space of the airport. As the film *The Terminal* suggests, borders can be constraining but it is their management that produces seemingly ridiculous displays of sovereign power. Second, we reflect on one material manifestation of border management – the checkpoint. In the Palestinian film *Divine Intervention*, it is the checkpoint and the Israeli border guards who are critical in managing mobilities in and around the border zone. The third example addresses border entanglements – demarcation and management. Using *Traffic* we consider how drugs, people and the border are connected to US/Mexican relations, the nuclear family and the drug-dependent nature of parts of US society.

The Airport and the Bordered Individual

Borders represent not only sites of sovereign power but also sites of resistance, subversion and transgression. When borders are violated then, it can cause a profound sense of crisis for a state and its population. In the aftermath of the September 11th 2001 attacks, airports within the United States were shut down and flights entering the country were diverted.

When airports re-opened, security measures were noticeably heightened with new restrictions placed on hand luggage and more pointed questioning at immigration control regarding visitors' travel plans within the United States. The state, in this case the US, sought to re-impose itself, especially at the border (which, of course, is not always to be found simply at the 'edges' of a state's territory).

In the comedy-drama *The Terminal*, the airport as a space of ambiguous sovereignty is explored through tracing the dramatic experiences of a man trapped in New York's JFK international airport. He is denied entry into the United States and at the same time he cannot return to his native country because of a sudden revolution. He is, in effect, imprisoned in the airport, subject to the capriciousness of events and procedures both there and further afield. The film itself was inspired by the real-life experiences of a young Iranian refugee called Mehran Karimi Nasseri who was a long-term resident at Charles de Gaulle international airport in Paris between 1988–2006. The border, as manifested within the airport, is a site and space of struggle over identity and belonging.

The film opens with officials from US Customs and Border Protection, preparing for newly arriving visitors. As the passengers arrive, they are asked the usual questions: 'what is the purpose of your visit?' and 'what are your travel plans?' In the control room, the airport security staff monitor the unfolding movements of the passengers. Victor Navorski (Tom Hanks), from the fictional country of Krakozhia, discovers on his arrival, that his country of origin has been overthrown by a revolution and that this act has invalidated the status of his passport. He is taken away from immigration control and questioned in a side room. He eventually meets Frank Dixon (Stanley Tucci), the head of US Customs and Border Protection at the airport.

Through his limited understanding of English he finally learns the consequences of the coup in Krakozhia: he is now both stranded and stateless. Dixon tells him: 'The State Department has revoked your visa, which was going to allow you to enter the United States.' The invalidated status of his passport, which a state is of course not obliged to issue (and can take back as well), exposes a powerful fiction contained within the front page of this document, namely the 'request in the name of Krakozhia to all those whom it may concern to allow the bearer to pass freely without let or hindrance and to afford him/her every assistance and protection of which he/she may stand in need'. As Victor learns to his apparent cost, when the authority of the issuing state disappears so does that explicit commitment. Victor's arrival in effect brings into formal existence a relationship between two sovereign states – Krakozhia and the United States and not Victor and the United States. And even then there is no automatic right of entry. As Dixon tells him, 'You don't qualify for asylum, refugee status, temporary protective status, humanitarian parole, non-immigration, work travel or diplomatic … you are at this time unacceptable. You have fallen into a small trap in the system.' Victor has exposed the limits of the classification system deployed by the state to regulate 'aliens'.

Thus, as a stateless person, Victor is trapped – he cannot enter or leave the United States. However, he is allowed to enter 'the international transit lounge' (a very particular kind of 'space', highlighted by the Edward Snowden affair and his prolonged stay at Moscow airport). Upon entering, he is given some food tokens, a calling card and a pager, which he is told he must keep with him at all times. He is also reminded that he is not to leave the transit lounge – 'America is closed'. Within the lounge, he learns via television news that his country has indeed been overrun by a *coup d'état*. Unable to phone home, due to his lack of understanding of how an English-language phone card works, he begins to explore the geographical parameters of the international transit lounge and discovers some of the areas he cannot access such as the members-only 'red carpet club'. With no social security to hand, or any other kind of support system, Victor is dependent on his own powers of

Securing the border through surveillance in *The Terminal*

improvisation, whilst constantly under the gaze of the surveillance cameras throughout the airport, closely monitored by Dixon and his colleagues.

His encounters with flight attendant Amelia (Catherine Zeta-Jones) and airport employee Enrique (Diego Luna) are critical in helping him to endure the privations of the airport, especially when Dixon is determined to monitor and admonish him for circumventing the airport's established order of things such as discovering that it is possible to make money by returning abandoned airport trolleys to an allotted zone. As time passes, Victor is dependent on television news to keep him informed of the state of his home country. He continues to try and enter the United States and is repeatedly told that his visa will not be issued until his country is officially recognised. At various times Dixon attempts to resolve the 'problem of Victor'. In one such attempt, Dixon is keen to pursue the possibility of Victor obtaining asylum status in a deliberate attempt to seek some kind of sanctioned resolution. Victor is told that he could be released from the airport if he can establish a 'credible fear' of persecution in his home country. Victor tells Dixon that he is more afraid of 'the room' he is in at present rather than his home country. He behaves in a manner that Dixon cannot comprehend – rather than seek to 'work' state bureaucracy he takes the various elements of state power at apparent face value.

After nine months living in the airport, the war in Krakozhia is finally declared over and Victor should now be allowed to leave the airport and finally enter the United States. With Amelia's help, Victor has secured an emergency travel visa to enter the United States – but it has to be signed by Dixon. Dixon refuses to entertain any such suggestion and tells Victor that 'my authority over this airport is absolute'. He wants to deport Victor for his exposing of airport security and procedures to ridicule. Out of spite, Dixon also threatens to deport and/or sack his friends at the airport for their support of Victor. With the help of some friends who delay the flight to Krakozhia, Victor confronts the security officers at the exit of the airport. In a gesture of solidarity with his plight, they refuse to arrest him. Victor is thus able to leave the terminal building and enter the United States, and fulfil the original purpose of his visit – to collect the autograph of a jazz saxophonist, which he needs to complete his recently-deceased father's dream of having all 58 autographs of the musicians featured in a Hungarian newspaper photograph in 1958. Then, rather than remain in the United States, Victor returns home to Krakozhia.

The Terminal, at its best, serves as a powerful reflection of how sovereign power is performed in an enclosed and highly securitised space. The airport building is perhaps the apogee of the national security state. It is at the border, as epitomised by the passport control point, where state-sanctioned agents make potentially life-changing decisions. It is at that point that the mobility of the individual is interrogated and needs to be defended. The figure of Dixon in this film illustrates well the precariousness of the traveller – in this case Victor. The disciplinary effect of the airport and its associated security practices on citizens is striking and the manner in which visitors can be summarily deported even when the documents, passport and travel story align with one another. Until those state-sanctioned agents accept our status our existence is precarious, as Victor discovered; more so, as the film suggests, if you come from a fictional yet unstable country such as Krakozhia, which is clearly modelled on a former Soviet Republic. Victor's nine-month sojourn in New York JFK's international airport is a direct consequence of the country's geopolitical instability and his unsteady status as a citizen. As Tim Cresswell notes, 'very few places are more finely differentiated according to the kinetic hierarchy than an international airport … airports and air travel in general are replete with stories of comfort, illness, pampering and torture – bodies stopped and examined interminably' (2006: 224). But there is also an issue regarding how borders are made and remade in particular sites, and the airport is one of those areas where the state and state-sanctioned authorities rehearse and perform the categorisation of the national and the international.

Checkpoints and Hyper-regulated Life

In both Israeli and Palestinian cinema, there are many examples of films made in the last decade or so which centre on the border and checkpoint itself. This is perhaps not surprising in the light of *intifadas*, the construction of the so-called 'security barrier' comprised of concrete walls and electrified fences, the disputed status of Jerusalem and the contested legality of settlements. Palestinian territories, especially in the West Bank, are also subject to ever-more stringent security checks, while Israeli settlement and associated infrastructure has intensified and magnified. Palestinian films have frequently highlighted the brutality of the occupation, including urbicide and the daily humiliation endured by Palestinians seeking to cross the border, in both directions, with Israel (see Graham 2004; Gregory 2004; Weizman 2007).

As a consequence, the 'border' has emerged as a highly material and symbolic manifestation of this occupying presence with its associated infrastructure, including the checkpoint. Israeli soldiers and border patrol officers have, within their possession, the power to make life-changing judgements concerning border crossings. In Giorgio Agamben's terms, it is they who possess sovereign power in an everyday context – they are guided both by national law but also by discretionary judgement. They may well be constrained by a chain of command but ultimately it is their interpretation that counts. It is the border guard, as many of these films including *Divine Intervention* suggest, who have the authority to sort, define and restrain/exclude people and vehicles from entering and leaving the West Bank and Gaza. As Nurith Gertz and George Khleifi claim, 'the borders have thus become a sign of oppression characterised by an Israeli definition of Palestinian as a non-existent, split or broken identity. This, perhaps, may explain why so many new Palestinian films take place at borders and checkpoints, and have therefore been termed "roadblock movies"' (2005: 324).

Elia Suleiman's *Divine Intervention* is a farcical comedy, which uses a series of brief and barely inter-connected sketches of everyday life in the West Bank. It is described as 'a chronicle of love and pain'. For the first thirty minutes or so of the film there is no depiction of the border, let alone any checkpoint itself. It opens with a man dressed as Father Christmas (George Ibrahim) running away from a group of children; he is dropping presents in his haste to escape and eventually we see that a knife is embedded in his chest. Thereafter, a whole series of static encounters are narrated including a man sitting at his breakfast table carefully sorting his post (it appears that he is ignoring bills) to another episode of a woman complaining about her neighbour throwing his rubbish into her garden, on a near daily basis. Another vignette features an old man convinced that a small road that   runs past his house is intruding on his property and so dismantles part of the offending structure.

While there are truly hilarious moments where spoken dialogue is kept to a minimum, such as the man who blows up a tank by throwing out of the window the discarded stone from a peach, these encounters emphasise torpidity, claustrophobia and casual violence. The everyday quarrels between neighbours involve an almost obsessive attention to one's land, and that – in this claustrophobic reality – border control takes on an added salience. The distinction between inside and outside is conducted on a daily basis, beyond the checkpoint, through the material infrastructure of the inhabitants in Palestinian towns and villages. Life is literally bordered. Suddenly, after these banal representations of everyday life in a West Bank town, the checkpoint appears in the film. There is a guard shouting at a taxi driver and other waiting vehicles hoping to cross into Israel. They are all told to turn around. Close to the actual checkpoint, a guard tower has been erected to facilitate surveillance of the waiting cars and surrounding area. Indeed, the checkpoint and guard post are located on open ground in order to prevent any surreptitious movement. While the armed guards ensure that the Palestinian drivers carry out their instructions, a young woman driving a car pulls up short of the checkpoint and continues on foot to the border. The soldiers warn her to go away and point their weapons at her. Such is her confidence and nonchalance, she continues walking without any restraint. Such is her poise the soldiers appear transfixed and as she crosses the guard tower collapses in an undignified heap – the impotence of the border and its paraphernalia exposed. The Al-Ram checkpoint, between Jerusalem and Ramallah, has been breached. For all their masculine bravado, a beautiful young woman has, in effect, ridiculed their attempts to securitise the border, and exposed the way in which sovereignty and security are frequently conceived as needing protection from masculine protectors epitomised by the figure of the border guard.

For others who wish to cross the checkpoint, the experience is not quite so simple. The two main characters in the film are a young couple, divided by several checkpoints. He lives in Jerusalem and she comes from Ramallah and they meet at the border zone in their separate cars. Once parked up, they sit in one car and the camera closely follows their expressions of intimacy, restricted simply to the touching of their hands. From their vantage point, however, they are able to see first-hand the physicality of the checkpoint. For example, a white van approaches the wooden and brick structure and associated barrier which makes up the checkpoint, and the armed soldiers demand that the driver and passengers open their doors, show their ID, declare their destination and then are ordered to turn around. As the couple sit in the car, darkness envelopes the checkpoint and powerful searchlights help to illuminate the checkpoint and survey the surrounding area. They watch three other men being forced to put their hands up so that they can be checked and their vehicle inspected. Simultaneously, a car pulls up sharply and three Israeli soldiers jump out and scrape their boots carefully – with the inference that they did not want to carry any trace of the 'West Bank', including its dirt, into Israel.

In that instant, the realities of border control are brought to the fore in their varied visual manifestations as it seeks to control, order and regulate space. It is a space of performance, as both the soldiers and those wishing to cross the border play their roles perpetuating forms of behaviour associated with obedience and deference. For their part, those that cross have to supply relevant documentation and 'behave' in a suitably pliant and non-threatening manner. The scraping of the shoes reminds us of how border discourses are so often associated with ideas of purity/dirt, inside/outside and identity/difference (see, for example, the extended discussion in Cresswell 1996). While the border connects, it also unwittingly raises the spectre of contamination and violation. Finally, we learn nothing about the lives of the soldiers and the civilians trying to cross the border. In a curious sort of way all those concerned are trapped, at least in those instances, by this small zone. The soldiers simply follow their orders and those trying to cross have to follow the orders originating from the soldiers.

In one of the funniest moments of the film, one of the key Palestinian characters releases a red balloon embossed with the smiling face of Yasser Arafat from his car and it subsequently travels towards the checkpoint. While the soldiers are checking the ID of another driver, they suddenly notice the balloon floating towards the border crossing. The balloon's mobility stands in sharp contrast to the earth-bound residents stuck at the checkpoint. The balloon's cross-border journey continues towards Jerusalem, as the soldiers dither. As Elia Suleiman noted himself about the balloon, 'The soldier in the roadblock can catch me, but he cannot capture my imagination … you don't need an identity card or passport to cross the border in your imagination' (cited in Gertz and Khleifi 2005: 333). And the point is that, in this film, the mundane object of the balloon (with the embossed face of Arafat) not only works imaginatively but also materially in reminding audiences that visual transgressions unsettle the claims of state to be able to survey and to intervene in the name of controlling their national territories. After passing a variety of religious buildings, the balloon becomes caught up on the Dome of the Rock – the third holiest-

A balloon floats across a checkpoint in *Divine Intervention*; Suleiman claims 'you don't need a passport to cross the border in your imagination'

place to Muslims and an enduring symbol of Jerusalem's status as a multi-cultural and multi-religious centre.

The final part of the film returns to the checkpoint and again the couple sitting in the car witness an Israeli solider humiliating a group of Palestinians as they attempt to cross the border. With the aid of a mega-phone, he orders the drivers to turn off their engine, show their ID and to get out of their cars. He takes a jacket from one driver and mocks them for wanting them to go to Jerusalem to break their fast, as it is Ramadan. After the mockery, he sings 'Long live the people of Israel'. He then orders them all to go on their way. As if to emphasise the broader qualities of the wider Israeli-Palestinian struggle, the film concludes with a series of emblematic symbols of resistance with a woman throwing stones in the face of five Israeli soldiers practising their shooting skills. The film's elegiac ending seems in keeping with a film dedicated to exploring the micro-geographies of the checkpoint and the power-geometries of the border.

Palestinian films such as *Divine Intervention* and more recent releases such as *Paradise Now* alongside Israeli productions such as *Machssomim* (*Checkpoint,* 2003) have helped propel into wider public consciousness the visibility of the checkpoint and border practices (again, see Gertz and Khleifi 2007). The checkpoint and its associated disciplinary practices serve as a visual anchor linking the unequal political geographies of mobility and control, and remind us how these particular sites help to visually and materially constitute state power. Crudely speaking, it is Israelis who get to travel quickly and relatively easily through checkpoints and border crossings and Palestinians who endure uncertainty and humiliation as they seek to negotiate scores of checkpoints around the West Bank. *Divine Intervention* suggests that there is something rather degrading about these practices even if it remains possible for love and the imagination to transgress the borders and boundaries erected by states and their functionaries.

Border Entanglements

Traffic offers rich potential for exploring how border control provokes a series of anxieties ranging from trans-national crime to teenage drug use and the stability of the Mexican state itself. This award-winning film featuring Michael Douglas, Benicio Del Toro and Catherine Zeta-Jones considers how the drugs trade co-implicates people, places and government agencies as they either attempt to control or profiteer (or both) from the presence of the border. Here, the border and borderlands both facilitate and restrict the movement of people and substances, and its existence attracts a premium in terms of the pricing and market availability of illegal materials. The border, in this case, is a bridge connecting supply areas south of the Rio Grande to demand areas in the United States, way beyond the immediate border regions. As if to emphasise these connections, the film's narrative is based in multiple locations from Mexico City and Tijuana to San Diego, Columbus, Cincinnati and Washington DC. Interspersed within the film are scenes from specific checkpoints, allowing the viewer to gaze at waiting cars seeking to cross north and south of the border, without dwelling on the actual experiences of border processing.

As with earlier border films in the 1980s, *Traffic* is in part a filmic reflection on the place of the border within contemporary neo-liberal globalisation. Released in 2000, it appears at the end of Bill Clinton's two-term presidency. Clinton in particular was a keen champion of economic forms of globalisation and argued that, alongside the spread of liberal democracy, there was the hope of a more pacific future. Clinton was also instrumental in establishing the North American Free Trade Association (or NAFTA) that liberalised trade between the US, Mexico and Canada. However, notwithstanding his apparent commitment to open markets and neo-liberal globalisation, concern over borders had not disappeared, as the onset of the War on Drugs would seem to testify in the 1990s. American forces were stationed in countries such as Columbia and participated in patrols of the Caribbean as part of attempts to prevent drugs entering the United States. What became apparent is that a public commitment to open borders and the free movement of people, ideas and goods was increasingly double-edged – while some flows might be welcomed, such as legitimate financial investment and skilled professionals, others, such as illegal immigrants and drugs, were less desired by national administrations including Clinton's. Border films of the 1990s and early 2000s such as *Traffic* and *Blow* (2001), using drugs as the object of concern, explore the multi-faceted nature of the border in an era of so-called intense globalisation.

The film works through a series of separate, yet ultimately connected, narrative strands. The opening scene (and first strand) features two local Mexican police officers close to the Californian border about to make a drugs bust. As with other parts of the film featuring Mexico, the background light is filtered and almost bleached by sun. The cops sit in their car surrounded by desert as if suggesting that the empty landscape itself unwittingly creates opportunities for the drugs trade. A plane carrying drugs lands somewhere close by. Just as they arrest the passengers of a suspect vehicle sent to recover the contraband, Mexican troops led by General Salazar (Tomas Milian) intercept them and take the truck into their possession. As the narrative makes clear, the Mexican military and legal infrastructure is portrayed as either deeply corrupt or simply unable to confront the main drug cartels. The two police officers are in effect recruited by Salazar, and told to destroy the Tijuana cartel. As the film progresses, Salazar is appointed head of an anti-drug taskforce in Mexico City while at the same time remaining complicit with a drug cartel.

The second strand involves a high-profile judge working in the United States, at the Ohio Supreme Court, first seen presiding over a drugs-related case involving a man planting drugs on his farm. While his teenage daughter is at home with friends 'experimenting' with drugs, the Judge is appointed as leader of the Office of the National Drug Control Policy. His portfolio involves taking control of US drugs policy and in particular the so-called War on Drugs. In a poignant moment, on the eve of his appointment, he is told at a reception held in the exclusive Georgetown district of Washington DC that 'Mexico-bashing is not going to make a damn difference'. Young people, such as his daughter Caroline, unbeknown to him, have easy access to drugs and at least 25 per cent of American teenagers might be involved with such substances. The judge finally learns of his daughter's drugs use when she is arrested and detained overnight by the local police after she and her friends are seen dumping an overdosed friend outside a hospital in the early hours of the morning. The judge's daughter's drug habit is shown to exemplify the problem posed by demand for drugs and the manner in which this commodity weaves its way across a distant border in the south of the United States into the 'heartland' of the nation. As her addiction worsens, she is also the victim of sexual violence. As Caroline later notes, while attending a rehabilitation clinic, it is easier for young people to buy drugs than alcohol – the former may be illegal but dealers do not care about the age of their customers (and they do not check IDs).

The third strand features two US cops working initially on a drugs bust in San Diego. In the midst of a shoot-out, they manage to apprehend Eduardo Ruiz (Miguel Ferrer), an associate of a major drugs baron, transferring merchandise from Mexico across the border to San Diego. While being questioned, he reminds the two detectives about the state of the border and the manner in which the North American Free Trade Agreement of 1994 has made it harder for law enforcement. As Eduardo opines, 'NAFTA makes this more harder [for law enforcement] because the border is disappearing … Mexican trucking companies will have the same freedom as UPS, DHL and FedEx'. Thousands of vehicles cross the US/Mexican border every day and no state (not even the US) has the resources to check every passenger and vehicle. As he tells the officers, 'We used regression analysis to calculate the odds of being stopped at the border … 'law enforcement is an entrepreneurial activity in Mexico … [and the *coup de grace*] Your government surrendered this war [on drugs] a long time ago.' He is later assassinated before he is able to testify against his former employer but before doing so reminds the federal officials sent to protect him that by arresting him they also 'work for the drug dealers too'. His untimely death enables his former employer to escape prosecution.

The fourth strand involves the wife of a major drug baron in San Diego who until his arrest has no awareness of his illicit activities. It is left to her husband's lawyer to enlighten her. As he whispers to her, 'He was very good at his job … smuggling illegal drugs into this country.' Her story becomes one of survival as she seeks to pay off a $3million debt to drug creditors and protect her child from the consequences of her husband being indicted for drug-related activities. It is she, as a white woman driving an expensive SUV, who crosses the border with ease in order to negotiate new drug-running opportunities. Her husband may be in jail but once she gains access to his multiple offshore bank accounts, she is able to re-capitalise and re-build his cross-border activities. With the co-operation of her cross-border partner, she proposes another drugs project called 'Project for the Children', which will see 'odourless and undetectable' cocaine-constructed dolls cross from Mexico to the United States.

The four strands criss-cross one another throughout the film and in some cases the characters cross the border simultaneously, albeit going in opposite directions. Underlying the film is a searing critique of US policy, especially the War on Drugs, which is shown to be ineffectual. After being appointed the new head of the anti-drugs task force, the judge visits the US/Mexican border at San Ysidro. He laments that, 'I am tired of talking to experts who have never left the beltway. It is time to see the frontiers.' On arrival, he is told about the scale of the issue – 45,000 vehicles and 20,000 pedestrians cross this border point every day. So as Eduardo noted earlier, it is impossible for all passengers and vehicles to be stopped and checked. Recently, a border official told him that drug seizures have increased threefold but at least 40–50 per cent of the total drugs smuggled over the border would be undetected. When he visits the El Paso Intelligence Center, he is informed that fifteen different agencies are involved in surveying and intervening in the drugs trade. Despite the impressive infrastructure, the officials are candid about the state of the border and the capacity of these agencies to regulate flows of drugs and people. As one official informs the judge, the drug cartels have unlimited resources and the US authorities cannot compete in terms of budgets. He is also told that Mexico does not have someone in his equivalent position. This is later to change when he meets General Salazar in Mexico City and both men talk about the possibilities for further co-operation, albeit with rather different priorities and vested interests. Salazar has no interest in the problem of addiction and the management of demand. On the plane home he tells his team that 'We need to take down one of those cartels.'

The judge clearly forgot the advice of those drugs experts in Washington about avoiding 'Mexican-bashing'. It seems that visiting the border has only served to reinforce old discourses and practices associated with the 'war on drugs'. Against this backdrop of policy inertia, his daughter

Caroline (Erika Christensen) and her boyfriend travel into the predominately African-American inner-city of Cincinnati for further drug supplies. Once drugs cross the US/Mexican border they are, with the help of cartel-based infrastructures, able to enter into US cities hundreds of miles from border locations such as San Diego and El Paso. And in so doing they connect the lives of wealthy white American teenagers to an underclass of African-American men, making a living selling drugs in rundown 'rust-belt cities' and elsewhere. Caroline's friend lectures the judge, both making reference to an 'unbeatable market force', and reproducing the kind of racist judgements that equates all young black men as potential drug dealers.

The final part of the film is unquestionably the bleakest. The drug cartels are not only shown to be ruthless but also capable of ingenuity and rapid flexibility (they are 'foot-loose', quite literally). Drug cartels, as with other non-state actors, not only have more resources than the state, but also actually possess a network-like organisation that can embed itself structurally inside cities and circumvent state authorities by bribery, violence and volume of traffic. By way of contrast, US state-based agencies are either rooted in place (for example, particular border crossings which are well known and identified) or slow to react to the changing nature of the cartel networks and leadership. The film ends on a mixed note. The judge discovers his daughter being exploited as a semi-comatose prostitute in a cheap hotel. Later at a press conference, the judge fails to complete his briefing to the press on the president's War on Drugs strategy. As he notes before leaving the public stage, 'I don't know how you wage war on your own family?' The corrupt General Salazar is eventually arrested and dies of a deliberate drugs overdose. The police officer based in San Diego, after losing his partner via a car bomb explosion, manages to plant a listening device in the home of the recently-freed drug baron and his wife. While the film does not dwell on the point, the act seems to suggest that the struggle to bring him and his cartel to justice will prevail. Javier (Benicio Del Toro), the Mexican police officer initially recruited by Salazar, plays a key role in his indictment and features in the final scenes of the film, watching children playing baseball. As Javier tells two DEA officials, 'Everyone loves baseball.' It is not clear whether Javier has been able to make a new life in America.

Traffic is a complex film, which highlights how the presence of the border can produce a series of entanglements, some of which have disastrous consequences. Lives are lost and shattered as a consequence of drugs. By the end of the film, it is clear that the drugs trade will not be altered let alone controlled by the border – better management is not the answer. As long as the border exists in combination with the premium that is attracted to an addictive and lucrative product, there will always be cartels willing and able to meet the demand in places like Cincinnati from all sections of society including privileged white upper-class Americans. Declaring 'war' on drugs is futile and self-defeating, as the 'war' on terror would be years later. The border produces unequal geographies and, per-haps, the drugs trade like capitalism more generally thrives in terms of product sourcing and market creation.

Visualising Border Practices

Borders have long been seen as a fundamental component of the interna-tional state system. Indeed, the founding of the modern system of state territoriality and sovereignty is normally traced to the Treaties of Westphalia in 1648. The creation of fixed borders (in which regard this treaty was a significant step) was a crucial element in the development of modern state sovereignty, gradually replacing a much more chaotic system of overlap-ping and discontinuous sovereignties and borders that had characterised medieval Europe. Borders, then, whilst often overlooked or neglected in the field of international relations, are the foundations of the international state system, without which the demarcation between the domestic and the international would not be possible. Such distinctions also happen, of course, in film studies, largely around debates on 'national cinemas' (although see Higbee and Lim 2010 for a review of the notion of 'transna-tional cinema').

Too often in the study and practice of international relations, the *fact* of 'the border' has been taken as unproblematic. Whilst the precise *loca-tion* of one border or another is recognised as historically contingent, the existence, form and function of borders *per se* nevertheless remains taken for granted. Such resolutely material understandings of the border (in the sense that only the material reality of the border is recognised) have increasingly been critiqued by post-structuralist accounts of borders. These accounts contend that political institutions (including 'the border') are both materially and discursively produced. Drawing on Deleuze and

Guattari, for example, Keith Woodward and John Paul Jones attempt to 'rethink the border outside of ideational/material preoccupations' (2005: 236) by refusing to prioritise either the 'real, material' properties of borders, or the 'ideational', 'metaphoric' and 'discursive' accounts of bordering that characterises much postmodernist thought.

The border film might be thought of as having made two key contributions to such a task. First, a critical reading of the genre can contribute towards a recognition of the discursive and conceptual construction of the border. As viewers and critics, we need to ask questions about the boundary-drawing practices of film itself – the ways in which particular narratives, editing devices and filmic techniques contribute to the construction of borders, boundaries and distinctions. Here one might think of the arguments made by proponents of 'critical geopolitics', that 'both the material borders at the edge of the state and the conceptual borders designating this as a boundary between a secure inside and an anarchic outside are objects of investigation... States are not prior to the inter-state system but are perpetually constituted by their performances in relation to an outside against which they define themselves' (Ó Tuathail and Dalby 1998: 3–4). We must attend, therefore, to a critique of the 'perpetual constitution' of such an inside/outside distinction, including the performance of such distinctions throughout popular culture.

Second, the films discussed in this chapter make visible the continual making, and remaking, of the border. The border is not a fixed line in the sand – rather it marks a terrain of contestation, management, control, resistance, power, technology and subversion. People and objects move through these borders in all kinds of ways for all manner of reasons. The selected films clearly do not exhaust the manifest ways that borders in the broadest sense have been examined by a variety of 'national cinemas'. However, as Tom Conley (2007) has noted, film itself is a territorial medium, which 'borders' in a variety of ways, ranging from the field of the image (that which the camera frames and allows the viewer to see) to the way in which film narratives invite viewers to locate themselves in a variety of border spaces, some of which may not have been physically encountered before. But as these films in their different ways suggest, the experiences of the border and the checkpoint in particular can be very different. The border as a line of division and control creates a series of complex geographies of exploitation and opportunity. People and commodities, such as drugs, play their role in sustaining and exploiting borderline opportunities with the most vulnerable being those migrants seeking employment in the low-wage agricultural and sweatshop sector in the US.

The border is also a problem and source of danger/insecurity. But in their attempts to secure the border in the name of 'national security', the state and its functionaries such as border guards and police officers often become embedded in a semi-permanent 'state of exception' (see the next chapter on 'exceptional spaces'), which appears to legitimate and justify torture, extra-judicial killing and extortion. The border itself is the problem. It is the border, and the narratives that surround it, which demarcate lines that seem to demand constant policing and vigilance. For students of international politics, 'border films' remind us that the border, considered to be central to claims pertaining to national sovereignty and international boundaries, is a human creation that can be built, contested and undone in a variety of settings.

A key feature of the contemporary border is the increasing use of technologies to control and regulate the flow of both bodies and objects across the border. Whilst all manner of border technologies are apparent in the three films discussed, it is in *The Terminal* that we perhaps see this issue brought most sharply into focus, with human actors working with and through such border technologies. Within this film we clearly see that the electronic database and biometric indicators are helping to re-constitute the figure of the border guard and the checkpoint. The regulation of the border is not so much about patrolling and protecting, as it is about making judgements about individuals based on their electronic footprints as well as their physical characteristics. Those kinds of judgements about borders and bordering also occur within borders as much as at those formal border points. Post-9/11, citizens were urged to become border guards inside the United States and report any suspicious individuals and activities. In response to such 'citizen-detective' programmes, not only in the US but also in the United Kingdom, Nick Vaughan-Williams talks of the 'generalised border', arguing that 'such practices, as a control on the movement of subjects, can be read as an attempted form of bordering not found at the outer edge of sovereign territory, but rather dispersed throughout society' (2008: 76).

Central to the dispersal of bordering practices throughout society, then, is a particular kind of 'watching', that Louise Amoore (2007), for example, has called 'vigilant visuality'. It is not just citizens, however, that engage in such visualities – the proliferation of cameras throughout Western society is also integral to this mode of watchfulness. Such forms of visuality are explored in films such as *Enemy of the State* (1998) and *Minority Report* (2002), as well as through the 'found footage' genre first made popular by *The Blair Witch Project* (1999) and used throughout *Cloverfield* (2008). And here we may return to (and indeed, finish with) an even more fundamental link between film and the border – the role of the camera itself as a key technology of surveillance. On one level, one could simply make the observation that the use of supposed security camera footage has become more commonplace in contemporary film. Indeed, Thomas Levin (2002) discusses how the use of surveillance footage has played a crucial narrative role in any number of recent films. Moreover, Levin uses this discussion not just to highlight a contemporary narrative technique within Hollywood film, but also to suggest that the use of such footage in movies contributes to a wider visual 'rhetorics of surveillance'.

For Levin, surveillance footage is predominantly used in film to provide an authoritative account of a particular event – shown in such a way that as viewers we are meant to take such footage as irrefutable proof that the events shown actually happened, rather than events taking place in the imagination of the characters, for example. He contends that such logic inevitably carries over into public debates and understanding of the wider role of CCTV in society. Thomas Mathiesen has taken the argument even further, writing back in 1987 that 'the greatly expanding mass media system provides the necessary belief context, the obedient, disciplined, subservient set of beliefs necessary for the surveillance systems to be functional' (1987: 75). Regardless of how far one is willing to accept such contentions, it is clear that with the likely continued proliferation of surveillance cameras, the relationship between all kinds of viewing practices and bordering practices require greater consideration.

3 EXCEPTIONAL SPACES

According to the Italian philosopher Giorgio Agamben, 'the state of exception, which was essentially a temporary suspension of the rule of law on the basis of a factual state of danger, is now given a permanent spatial arrangement, which as such nevertheless remains outside the normal order' (1998: 169). By drawing upon the work of Michel Foucault and Carl Schmitt, Agamben contemplates a bio-political structure of sovereign power. This 'state of exception' is theorised as being enabled by the sovereign who possesses the power to suspend the law and establish at the same time a new legal-judicial order with a sharply defined inside and outside. Sovereignty defines and limits the law, where emergency powers in force have the capacity to reduce citizens to bare life. In *State of Exception* (2005), Agamben considers further how the suspension of the rule of law and the state of exception has become increasingly normalised and no longer considered both an emergency and/or exceptional measure.

In the aftermath of the September 11th 2001 attacks, Agamben's thoughts on the 'state of exception' have enjoyed considerable exposure within the social sciences and humanities, as the United States and other countries claimed exceptional powers in the face of the threat of global terrorism. It has been contended that the creation of emergency powers has helped to initiate a constant state of exception not only at the border but also within national territories themselves. As Agamben warns, the state of exception is a zone of *indistinction* where the law is held in abeyance and emergency powers become the norm (a film such as *District 9*

(2009) arguably deals with such issues, even if through the use of allegory). It becomes, in short, the dominant paradigm of government (see Agamben 2005: 2). At its worst, it is the return of the camp that illustrates the excesses of sovereign power; the detention camps within the US Naval Station at Guantánamo Bay and Abu Ghraib prison in Iraq being perhaps the most notorious examples. As Agamben claims, 'the camp is the space that is opened when the state of exception begins to become the rule of law' (1998: 168–9).

In recent years, geographers and other scholars have charted the exponential growth in exceptional measures and practices, with their distinct geographies ranging from biometric security checks at airports to so-called black sites and beyond. Joined with an interest in what Foucault termed 'biopolitics', the contemporary national security state is increasingly noted to be preoccupied with managing populations through surveillance, monitoring and policing of public spaces. In this politically altered landscape, film has played its part in visualising these varied biopolitical and exceptional geographies, and arguably re-casting the visual horizon of viewers. This becomes all the more important when we consider films such as *Rendition* released in a post-Abu Ghraib era, which exposed US complicity in war crimes. More generally, it reminds us that state power partly rests on a capacity to make visible some objects and people and to hide others.

The first film to be considered here, then, is *Rendition*, a film about the spatial and political arrangements associated with the practices of extraordinary rendition. The narrative arc takes in a variety of places including a fictional North African state, and the cities of Chicago, Cape Town, Cairo and Washington DC. It invites the viewer to both feel the pain of the racial other, while at the same time using particular white Americans to offer up redemptive possibilities for the United States. There are, as a consequence, particular embodied subject positions that are brought to the fore. Second, we consider a pre-9/11 movie, *The Siege*, which remains one of the most pertinent examinations of what happens when an entire city is turned into a space of exception following devastating attacks by unknown terrorists. It is through the intimate interaction of a close-knit group of FBI counter-terrorism officers that we learn as viewers how the state of exception not only differentiates but also subsequently might be reversed. Finally, the role of the exceptional figure is considered via *Iron Man*. The super-hero, in the form of industrialist Tony Stark (Robert Downey

Jr.), proves able and willing to confront terrorists directly and to operate beyond the law in domestic and external spaces for the purposes of confronting danger. He is, as Joshua Gunn (2008) has noted with reference to *War of the Worlds* (2005), a paternal sovereign who exercises exceptional powers, in an attempt to both redeem the United States in the case of Afghanistan while exposing the corrupt sectors of the military-industrial complex which would endanger the lives of Americans and Afghans.

An Exceptional Space: The Black Site

Using *Rendition*, we can profitably consider the role of so-called 'black sites' in the War on Terror and consider the geographies of brutality, compassion and shame via the fate of two families living in Chicago and North Africa respectively. Released in the final years of the two-term Bush presidency, it was a timely intervention in the sense of contributing to wider cultural debates about torture, complicity and national identity. In the midst of those discussions, Trevor Paglen (2007, 2009) released a series of publications detailing a global network of sites including multiple prisons, detention centres and airports used by the CIA to transport prisoners and suspected terrorists from Afghanistan and elsewhere around the world. Hundreds of so-called ghost prisoners have been transferred via this global prison system, which in turn enabled extraordinary rendition and torture – the illegal transfer of people from one state to another (see Gregory 2006). The location of these black sites has been a closely guarded secret, but a Council of Europe report (2006) helped to expose the US-led practice of rendition and the way in which places like Morocco, Syria, Uzbekistan, Jordan, Afghanistan and Guantánamo Bay were tied to these illicit flows.

Rendition features well-known Hollywood stars such as Reese Witherspoon, Jake Gyllenhaal, Peter Sarsgaard and Meryl Streep, and takes inspiration from the true story of Khalid El-Masri, a German citizen who was mistaken for Khalid al-Masri (a suspect named in the 9/11 commission report), and as a consequence was rendered to various torture sites across the globe before his eventual release. More directly, the film also draws upon the similar experiences of a Canadian-Syrian citizen, Maher Arar, who forms the basis of the fictional character Anwar El-Ibrahimi (played by Omar Metwally). Anwar, an Egyptian-born US citizen, lives in Chicago with his white middle-class wife, Isabella (Reese Witherspoon);

It is around these two that the narrative in *Rendition* revolves. The role of Isabella is central to the film, as Rachel Walsh (2011) has noted, because she orientates the viewer towards the plight of this Green Card-holding resident and his assimilation into American life. After a business trip to South Africa for the purpose of attending a conference, he fails to arrive in the United States as expected, having previously confirmed to his wife, through a phone call, that his plane will arrive in Chicago via Washington DC as scheduled.

The film then switches to 'North Africa', although no further detail is provided about the actual locations involved as if to emphasise the blurry and covert nature of the rendition programme. The precise location is not just withheld from the viewer, but also from Douglas Freeman (Jake Gyllenhaal), a young, white, CIA officer, who as the film develops performs a similar role to Isabella, in that both become central to shaping the narrative arc in ways that attempt to re-assert America's claims to compassion in the face of obvious brutality (see Walsh 2011). Later, as Freeman and a colleague, Dixon (David Fabrizio), drive to attend a meeting, a suicide bomber detonates a bomb, killing Dixon and many others in the city square. On hearing the news of the attack, a senior CIA official based in Washington DC orders Anwar to be picked up at a Washington airport. He is suspected of having been in contact with the assumed mastermind behind the attack. On arrival, Anwar is ushered into a secret room at the airport where he is immediately hooded, his baggage confiscated and his passenger record deleted from the manifest. He is then transferred to an interview room and interrogated by an official who claims that his mobile phone has incriminating phone numbers. He is then asked to list the people he met in Cape Town while being denied any contact with either his wife or lawyer. The interrogator notes that 'he has experience of explosives' as a consequence of his past involvement in explosive detection work for a US government agency.

His disappearance triggers a desperate search by Isabella who travels to Washington hoping for news of her missing husband. The senior CIA official handling the case, Corrine Whitman (Meryl Streep), is informed that Anwar has passed a polygraph test. She is dismissive and takes the fateful decision to 'put him on the plane', knowing that they cannot hold Anwar indefinitely in the United States. Bare life, as Agamben might have noted, began the moment he was dragged from the airport (see Danchev 2006).

A hooded Anwar arrives in an un-named North African country on a CIA-arranged rendition flight in *Rendition*

Freeman is told that 'he has a new detainee on the way' and that he is to observe the interrogation of Anwar when he arrives at a small airport. A hooded Anwar is immediately transferred to an army truck and taken to the interrogation centre. The film then switches to Isabella patiently waiting in Washington for a meeting with an old university friend, Alan, who is an aide to US Senator Hawkins (Alan Arkin). It is Alan who carefully explains the origins of rendition while walking with Isabella around Washington. This particular juncture of the film is important because it works to remind us of the often-gendered nature of national and international politics (both in practice and in representational form). Alan, as a kind of paternal guardian is in effect guiding Isabella through the complex spaces of counter-terrorism that does not always reflect the ideals of the nation. While Alan tells her that there is no record of Anwar ever boarding the aircraft, Isabella's insistence that a credit card charge of $70 seems to suggest that Anwar was actually on board the plane in question is all she can muster. An electronic trace hinting at an onboard transaction is all there is in terms of indicating the presence of Anwar, the same kind of trace often used by counter-terrorism officers to track and survey terrorist suspects. Alan agrees to help Isabella and asks for a meeting with the Senator. Although the film does not dwell on the point, it begs the question as to what would have happened if there had been no record of that credit card transaction because it is that mundane piece of evidence which proves crucial to Alan and Isabella's campaign to reveal Anwar's whereabouts.

As they consider their limited options in the bureaucratic snake-pit that is Washington, back in 'North Africa' Anwar is thrown into a small cell, Freeman meets the local intelligence chief, Abasi Fawal (Igal Naor), outside the detention centre; his complicity becomes clearer as the two shake hands and Freeman hands over a list of CIA-approved questions for Anwar. Fawal asks Freeman if he is going to stay for the interrogation and reminds him that he is there only to observe. Anwar is stripped of his clothing. He implores Fawal to allow him to speak to a lawyer. Anwar sees Freeman and asks him 'Are you American? I have lived in the States for twenty years. My wife is American.' He confirms that he was born in Egypt but came to America at the age of fourteen and studied at New York University. Fawal confronts him with telephone call evidence that suggests the mastermind contacted him from Egypt.

Fawal attempts to extract information from Anwar who is forced to defend the fact that he has regular contact with family relatives in Egypt. As the interrogation continues, Anwar learns that his professional background plus surname in addition to the previous telephone calls have implicated him in terrorism. Nothing he can say or do apparently makes any difference. A naked and chained Anwar is returned to a small dark cell. Back in Washington, Alan is talking with Senator Hawkins about Anwar and the practice of extraordinary rendition. Alan asks who would give the order for rendition. He is told 'Corrine Whitman'; the woman who is everything that Isabella is not – an older woman whose neo-conservative credentials seem deeply at odds with the younger liberal pregnant mother. Hawkins knows because he is a member of the Senate Intelligence Committee and is briefed weekly by Whitman. If Freeman is complicit with rendition in North Africa, men like Hawkins in Washington are also complicit. He was clearly not surprised by Alan's line of questioning in his office. As Alan later explains to Isabella,

> the CIA calls it extraordinary rendition. It started under Clinton. The Agency wanted to move suspected terrorists without having to formally apply for foreign extradition … it is supposed to be used only under extraordinary circumstances but after 9/11 it took on a whole new life. Basically the government has authorised the seizure and transfer of anyone they suspect of being involved in terrorism to secret prisons outside the US.

While Isabella has been given a lesson in post-9/11 counter-terror operations, a naked Anwar continues to be held in a darkened solitary cell, the clear victim of this change of policy post-9/11.

After a sustained period of torture, Anwar eventually 'confesses' to how he was offered $40,000 in return for advice on constructing more devastating bombs designed for terror attacks. Freeman, who is becoming increasingly troubled by the torture, asks Anwar to provide further details about how the money was transferred to him in South Africa. In desperation, Anwar reveals the names of supposed members of the terror cell. When Freeman does an Internet search, he discovers that Anwar has simply given him the names of past members of the 1990 Egyptian football team. Moreover, as Freeman asks, why would Anwar place his life and his family in jeopardy for a comparatively small amount of money given that his salary ($200,000 per year) is considerably higher? Convinced that Anwar is innocent, Freeman arranges for Anwar to be released from the prison. Back in Washington, Isabella finally confronts Whitman about her husband's disappearance. As she shouts at Whitman, 'you have my phone number, you have my home address, you have my husband ... just tell me where he is!', two security officers prevent Isabella from any further questioning.

Freeman is instrumental in securing Anwar's release and takes him from the prison. He arranges for Anwar to go covertly back to Chicago via Malaga and Madrid. With Anwar's experiences made public to the news media in the United States by Freeman, senior figures such as Whitman and others are forced to confront their complicity in the torture of Anwar. While the film centres our sympathies around Isabella, Anwar and Freeman, it never addresses the question of the telephone calls on Anwar's phone and whether it might have been possible for someone else to use the engineer's phone without his prior knowledge. We also learn little about the eventual fate of those implicated in the practice of rendition, especially in the United States.

However, *Rendition* does expose how Anwar, a highly educated and Green Card-holding US resident, was so quickly reduced to 'bare life' with no access to legal advice and judicial process – perhaps his fate is all the more shocking because he is so apparently 'integrated' into American life. The film ends with Anwar's return to Chicago and reunion with his wife and son outside their suburban house – in essence the promise of a multi-cultural and yet integrated vision of America has been restored to its proper place. By returning the now restored family, the film suggests, as Rachel Walsh (2011) notes, that 'America' can restore itself while reassuring the viewer that rendition and torture are exceptional practices that got out of control due to the over-zealousness of some officials in Washington and local accomplices. And by highlighting such practices, there is an implicit reminder to citizens that holding the state (and government officials) to account involves being able to see its excesses.

The City Under Siege

The Siege, starring Denzel Washington and Bruce Willis, is an example of a Hollywood film addressing terrorism that has garnered a great deal more attention post-9/11. The movie is perhaps notable in three main regards. First, it can now be seen as remarkably prescient, featuring as it does images of spectacular terrorist attacks in New York City, some three years before 9/11, when such scenes were likely to be considered somewhat fantastical (see Boggs and Pollard 2006). It has also taken on an additional sense of prescience in light of the Boston Marathon bombings of April 2013, depicting as it does the imposition of martial law within an American city in order to allow the authorities to apprehend a wanted terrorist. Second, the film has been widely discussed in relation to its portrayal of Muslims in general, and the Arab-American community in particular (see, for example, Mandel 2001). Third, attention has also focused on the way in which the city of New York, and in particular Brooklyn, became subject to the politics of exceptionalism in the aftermath of the series of devastating terrorist attacks that the film portrays. As such the film pre-figures many of the most contentious tactics and strategies pursued by the United States in the War on Terror, and at times enters into a discussion about appropriate responses to national security threats. This is achieved through the interplay of the four main American characters – two FBI officers, a CIA officer and an army general – as the film's narrative shifts from an attempt to treat the terrorist attacks as a criminal matter to an approach that favours extra-judicial and martial law.

The film's opening provides some context for that transformation of the legal and judicial process. A television report notes the death of US service personnel in Saudi Arabia believed to be the responsibility of terrorists. Subsequently, the terrorist leader is kidnapped and subject to extraordinary rendition (though this term, now part of the everyday language of the War on Terror, is never used in *The Siege*). With the help of satellite imagery, the viewer is able to follow the kidnapping operation somewhere, we later learn, in Lebanon. Thereafter, the movie shifts attention to New York with fleeting images of a mosque in Brooklyn and then to the counter-terrorism unit of the FBI. News breaks that terrorists have taken over a bus, and FBI officers including Anthony Hubbard (Washington) and Arab-American colleague Frank Haddad (Tony Shalhoub) have been called to the scene. It proves to be a hoax and the perpetrators leave a message, which gives little detail but stresses that there will be no negotiation. An Arab man, stopped at the airport, is tailed and judged to be suspicious because he has $10,000 in cash in his luggage. As he enters Brooklyn, the man in question continues to be followed and is later apprehended by an unidentified van operated by the CIA, led by Elise Kraft (Annette Bening). Within the first twenty minutes of the film then, CIA operatives have been shown, as Hubbard tells Kraft, to have been implicated in both kidnapping and assault.

Thereafter, the terrorist actions begin to escalate. As Hubbard and Kraft travel to the FBI headquarters, a second incident occurs involving a bomb planted on a commuter bus. The explosion leads to the deaths of 25 people (the 'worst bombing since the Oklahoma City attack' according to the fictionalised news reports within the film, which further state that 'Beirut came to Brooklyn today' – a proclamation that re-works the geographical imagination of Brooklyn as being transformed into a conflict zone). Further attacks soon take place as a lone gunman takes a group of schoolchildren hostage and a bomb explodes inside a theatre on Broadway.

In the midst of these attacks, we see the analysis room of the FBI headquarters, where computer screens are shown to be processing and evaluating streams of information including analysis of the explosives used. A link is found with the events with which the film opened – the attack on US personnel in Saudi Arabia and the consequent kidnapping of the terrorist leader. Thus Hubbard discovers via Kraft that 'the government is in the kidnapping business' and that the terrorist leader's capture might be key to the 'blowback' in Brooklyn. They discover that Samir (Sami Bouajila), a local college lecturer in Brooklyn, is key to the entry into the US of a series of young Arab men via sponsoring student visas.

The escalation in the terror attacks has a number of consequences. First, the failure of the civilian investigation (under the FBI) to apprehend the perpetrators leads to increasingly heated exchanges between the main protagonists. Kraft (CIA) and Hubbard (FBI), for example, repeatedly clash over procedure – she castigates him for working within the 'quaint laws' of the United States, he retorts that 'this isn't the Middle East' – in other words Brooklyn cannot become like Beirut. Beyond the individual criticism of Kraft, the film portrays a growing unease amongst civilians and the media with the handling of the crisis by the FBI. Second, ethnic and racial tension begins to increase across the city – television reports note a growing trend of violence directed towards Arab-Americans living in Brooklyn, and an inter-agency public meeting provides further 'evidence' of hardening attitudes towards immigrants as a 'culture of fear' begins to permeate the city. This 'fear of the other' finds its fuller expression later in the film with the establishment of makeshift detention camps for Arab-Americans.

It is in the face of this fear and anxiety about whether conventional law enforcement is sufficiently efficacious that a high-level meeting in Washington convenes to discuss future options. When asked about the potential role of the Army, General Devereaux (Bruce Willis) retorts: 'You do not want the Army in an American city … make no mistake we will find the enemy, we will kill the enemy [but] I implore you, do not consider this as an option.' Hubbard, meanwhile, reminds the meeting that 'you cannot fight a war against an enemy you cannot see … we [should] exercise patience and restraint'. The truck-bombing of the FBI headquarters occurs whilst this meeting is taking place. Frustrated at this incapacity to prevent further atrocities, the President declares martial law and the 101st Airborne Division enters New York and seals off Brooklyn in particular, because of its social and ethnic geography.

The following section of the film thus provides the viewer with an imagined 'space of exception' – a heavily-militarised zone in which all of the normal, civil laws have been suspended, where even the FBI and CIA officers have to move covertly around the city. Whilst previously displaying reluctance to mobilise his military forces, once commanded to do so by the President, General Devereaux fully commits to the imposition of martial law – tanks and soldiers patrolling the streets, the establishment of military checkpoints and the re-designation of Yankee Stadium as a makeshift detention camp for 'suspects'. As far as this military regime is concerned, any male of Arab-American origin is considered a 'suspect', including the

In images prescient of the military lockdown of Boston in 2013, Brooklyn is subject to military rule in *The Siege*

son of Frank Haddad, the FBI agent who partners Hubbard. At one point, Hubbard makes his way to Yankee Stadium to help arrange the release of Haddads' son. Haddad refuses Hubbard's offer, Frank stating: 'this is where I belong ... tell them [the FBI and Army] I am not their sand nigger anymore.' In protest at his son's treatment and that of Arab-Americans more generally, Frank quits the FBI.

The resolution of the film involves the hunting and capture of the chief suspect, Tariq Husseini (Amro Salama), a name given to Hubbard and Kraft after they visit Samir and demand his co-operation. Once captured, Husseini falls into the custody of General Devereaux who invokes the 'ticking bomb' scenario as a justification for using torture and violence against Husseini, against the protestations of Hubbard and his warning of the dire implications. Husseini's screams are heard and then finally a single shot – he has been killed. Despite the capture and murder of Husseini, the detentions and arrests continue unabated as the military personnel patrol the streets day and night. As they continue their investigations, Hubbard and Kraft's movements are continually monitored by the military. Nevertheless, they manage to once again track down Samir, and eventually discover that he is part of the terrorist cell planning and executing the attacks. In an ensuing struggle, Hubbard kills Samir but not before Kraft is herself killed. After the killing of Samir, Hubbard returns to confront Devereaux and places him under arrest for the torture and murder of Husseini and the kidnapping of the terrorist leader. The General orders his troops to turn their guns on the FBI officers and declares: 'I am the law. Right here, right

53

now. I am the law.' Hubbard retorts: 'You have the right not to be tortured, not to be murdered, rights that you took away from Tariq Husseini.' The General eventually desists and is arrested. Martial law is lifted and Haddad has an emotional reunion with his son. The film ends with detainees being reunited with their families and the army retreating out of the city.

The Siege, then, is an interesting film in a number of respects, not least because it appears to be remarkably prescient. Part of its prescience is in the imagining and visualising of a series of spectacular terrorist attacks on American soil. But perhaps what is more interesting is the way in which the film pre-figures the kinds of debates that would take place within America about how best to *respond* to the 'threat of terror'. In this respect *The Siege* can be understood as playing out opposing perspectives in these debates, with Hubbard representing those that would argue for the use of legal and civil means for protecting the homeland, and Devereaux representing the 'by any means necessary' approach. In this instance, 'by any means necessary' equates to the suspension of civil law and the creation of distinct spaces of exception *within* an American city.

Analysing the politics of *The Siege* in this regard is rather more complex than one might imagine. On the one hand, the film, it could be argued, works to normalise the exceptional – to make torture, rendition and the suspension of civil law appear as reasonable and possible responses to the 'threat of terror'. On the other, however, it is clear that the filmmakers want our sympathies to lie with Hubbard and the FBI, rather than with Devereux and the Army (or even Kraft and the CIA). The *dénouement* of the film, the confrontation between Hubbard and Devereaux, depicts a triumph of the rule of law – ultimately in the film, American values of justice, fair process and the primacy of the Constitution win out.

The politics of *The Siege* are also complex in the manner in which both 'Arabs' and 'terrorists' are depicted. As Carl Boggs and Tom Pollard note '*The Siege* departs from earlier terrorist-action plots owing to its more complex, nuanced range of narratives and motifs... [it] offers a far more variegated picture of Muslim terrorists and their cultural milieu than can be found elsewhere in Hollywood cinema' (2006: 343). In support of this claim they point to the way in which the terrorists, whilst always portrayed as 'the bad guys', are nevertheless provided with the opportunity to account for the actions in ways that often implicate US actions elsewhere in the world. Moreover, the film also depicts Arab-Americans as being the embodiment of the 'state of exception'. In this sense, the film has, within the narrative arc, a redeeming message of tolerance and respect. Indeed, Daniel Mandel shows how the filmmakers sought to 'head-off' any criticism of the film by the Arab-American community through a careful portrayal of the majority of Arab-Americans as loyal to the United States; 'the point is repeatedly made that a small, seditious minority is the problem, not Muslims and Arabs at large' (2001: 23). Nevertheless, the film does, of course, present the security threat to the United States as emerging from Islamic and Arab organisations and individuals. Mandel notes how despite the best intentions of the filmmakers, the Committee for American-Islamic Relations criticised the film for its portrayal of Arabs and Muslims in severe terms.

The Siege, then, is a noteworthy film, which considers how the fear of terrorism can be used to declare a state of emergency. The US Army deploys exceptional powers in the form of martial law, with disastrous consequences. Public space becomes militarised and the use of torture and killing is sanctioned by the emergency powers invested in the US Army. The character of Frank Haddad is particularly noteworthy – a man who has been apparently integrated into American society as demonstrated by his perfectly-spoken English and his job as a FBI officer – but he rapidly discovers that at a time of exceptional circumstances his loyalty and, by extension, that of his family is under suspicion. It is his character and Samir's that provide critical links with past episodes of US foreign policy in the Middle East, offering some insights as to why these attacks happened in the first place. While the FBI officers eventually overcome the General's command, the FBI have also shown themselves to be capable of killing terrorist suspects, albeit armed with warrants. In light of the Boston Marathon bombings of April 2013, debates about the use of exceptional measures in the name of homeland security have acquired a new urgency.

The Superhero and the State of Exception

Normal conventions and legal constraints appear immaterial to the superhero. From Superman to Captain America, the enduring presence of the superhero (usually male) suggests that the prevailing legal order cannot always adequately secure justice (see Dittmer 2005, 2011). In order to secure justice or otherwise, the superhero is required because s/he is able to operate beyond the law and this is made possible, in part, because they are tolerated, even encouraged, by grateful city authorities and/or national governments. Moreover, in order to be creditable, the superhero possesses some extraordinary abilities and powers such as flight, strength, resilience and determination. Their extra-judicial status is frequently reaffirmed by the presence of a mask – these are individuals who depend upon secrecy and discretion for their efficacy. If they must act outside the socio-legal order then they need to be freed from the demands of public scrutiny and accountability.

Iron Man, featuring Robert Downey Jr as Tony Stark, provides an illustration of how the role of the superhero is shaped by the state of exception. Stark, a child prodigy and owner of Stark Industries, is at the centre of the unfolding narrative. The opening part of the film offers glimpses into Stark's life as a brilliant designer, travelling with an army convoy in Afghanistan. The very weapons his company manufactured are used in a devastating attack on his convoy. Stark survives but is captured by his attackers. Earlier, his private jet transports him and the company's military liaison officer Colonel Rhodes (Terrence Howard) to Afghanistan in order to demonstrate Stark Industries' new weapon, the so-called 'Jericho' missile. What had started as a trip designed to show off the visually destructive power of the missile ends up being disastrous. As Jacques Derrida noted in the early 1980s, the missile acts as a 'missive' in sending a message to recipients regarding the capacity to deliver and dispatch these destructive objects (see Derrida 1983). Stark's hubris, and more generally that of America as well, was cruelly exposed in the deserts of Afghanistan.

Taken by his attackers, a terrorist group called 10 Rings, Stark discovers that he is now trapped in a cave somewhere in Afghanistan. A well-meaning colleague, Dr Yinsen (Shaun Toub), has kept him alive and embedded an electromagnet in his chest, which is critical to his survival. The terrorist leader orders Stark to make his group a Jericho missile. After initially refusing, he is tortured by the group. He is also shown evidence that the group already have a considerable stockpile of Stark Industries weapons. Unbeknown to his captors, despite their constant surveillance, Stark and Dr Yinsen actually build a suit of armour. After several months of activity, the terror group demand to see the end product. Determined to protect Stark and his creation, Dr Yinsen creates a diversion so that Stark can attempt an escape from the cave. After an intense fight, Stark manages to do so, whilst also managing to destroy the armed supplies of the terror group. After a short flight, Stark crashes in the desert and his suit appears to have been destroyed. He is eventually rescued by a US military helicopter crew including Colonel Rhodes and taken back to the United States.

It is upon his return that the main narrative arc of the film begins. His experiences in Afghanistan, together with the dying words of his saviour Dr Yinsen to 'not waste your life', lead to Stark re-evaluating his priorities. He decides that Stark Industries will no longer make weapons. As he tells an audience gathered to hear him speak upon his return, 'I came to realise that I have more to offer this world than things just to blow up ... I am shutting down the weapons manufacture division.' His business partner Obadiah Stane (Jeff Bridges) informs him that the board of directors will contest this decision.

In order to uphold his decision and to concentrate his energies on other projects, Stark aims to build *inter alia* a better version of his Afghan armour suit. While he is devising a new suit, the terror group discovers his former creation in the Afghan desert. His personal assistant, Pepper Potts (Gwyneth Paltrow), gives him a special miniature reactor encased in glass and bearing the inscription 'Proof that Tony Stark has a heart'. This gesture is important in securing the characterisation of Stark as a reformed arms manufacturer, re-positioning him as an innovator in new technology for civil purposes. Stane is determined, however, to continue with the production of Jericho missiles and, unbeknown to Stark, has been selling the missiles to the United States and insurgents in Afghanistan. The film thus begins to raise questions about the ethics of the global trade in arms, the connections between key industries in the US economy and global terror, and the possibilities of a more beneficent role for modern technology in international affairs.

The issue of 'humanitarian intervention' is soon added to the list of issues that the film addresses. Stark learns via television news reports that the situation in Afghanistan is deteriorating and that 'there is very little hope for refugees' because of a lack of will from the international community. This failure to protect becomes the test case for Stark's new found determination to confront the legacy of his company *vis-à-vis* weapons manufacturing. He decides to intervene for the benefit of Afghan refugees and dons his new suit and travels to Afghanistan. In particular, in a public acknowledgement of a debt he owes from his last visit to Afghanistan, he travels to the home village of Dr Yinsen and saves the village from the marauding forces of the 10 Rings. As he travels back towards the US, however, his trajectory is tracked by the US armed forces, and he is thus forced to reveal his identity to the US military. Stark tells them that he 'was just doing their [i.e. the US armed forces'] job'.

Once back in the US, Stark hacks into the Stark Industries computer in order to monitor recent shipments of weapons. It becomes clear to Stark that Stane hired the 10 Rings in an attempt to kill him. Moreover, Stane has returned to Afghanistan in order to take possession of the prototype 'Iron Man' suit, still held by the 10 rings terror group, which he does, after massacring the terrorists. Stane returns to the US, with the prototype suit, and the scene is thus set for the final showdown. Ostensibly this is between Stark's Iron Man and Stane's Iron Monger, but the showdown could also be read as one between competing visions of the role of the US in the world, embodied in these opposing assemblages of human and machine. The showdown unfolds in the roads and buildings close to Stark Industries. Military chiefs prevent the armed forces from scrambling jets to investigate the aerial confrontation between the two adversaries; Iron Man emerges as the victor, though not before the two men/machines have an opportunity to have a final conversation about the role of weapons and Stark's misguided idealism concerning the cessation of weapons production.

Throughout the film, Stark's inventiveness and presence of mind is not just tolerated by government agencies but also actively encouraged. His interventions in Afghanistan not only saved the life of one US pilot but also decisively intervened against a terror group, the 10 Rings who were responsible for the initial attack on Stark and his military convoy in Afghanistan. With his exceptional powers, Iron Man used the exceptional circumstances pertaining to Afghanistan to achieve exceptional results. *Iron Man* presents us with a story involving a good, successful white US citizen (Stark) responding to the pain of others including vulnerable Afghan citizens. Through his actions, Tony Stark has redeemed himself as a weapons manufacturer and also shown that his creative genius can be used positively both in Afghanistan and the United States. He may be a flawed genius, but he is a national subject who has, in an exceptional manner, achieved justice and redemption. American power can be used for the good of others. *Iron Man* serves as a kind of reverse *24*'s (2001–2014) Jack Bauer fantasy. If Bauer is the paternal sovereign that uses exceptional powers to protect America from its enemies then Tony Stark is the epitome of American technological prowess and cultural ideals – a lone ranger attentive to the consequences of unbridled violence. The politics here are complex though, for of course it is only through (technologically enhanced) violence and the use of powers and actions outside of the normal course of the law, that Stark, via Iron Man, is able to express these ideals.

Visualising Spaces of Exception

Amongst critical scholars, Agamben's corpus of work has been widely judged to be insightful in the ways in which it draws attention to how extraordinary powers work in a variety of geographical spaces, and in ways that are both hidden and visible. The films in question here help us consider some of the topographies of extraordinary power and the corresponding states of exception. The films discussed have brought to attention the different ways in which the exceptional materialises in particular places with very different kinds of consequences. For, as we have argued elsewhere, 'whilst it is possible to conceive of the "battlefronts" of the War on Terror as "de-territorialised", such an understanding must also retain an appreciation of the ways in which forms of violence and state power are nevertheless spatialised, and produce distinctive cartographies' (Carter and Dodds 2011: 107). Even if it does not precisely name them, a film like *Rendition* nevertheless works towards making such places and spaces of exception visible within the geopolitical imagination.

Moreover, given the very form of cinema itself, a form that, to varying degrees relies upon the principles of montage, films such as *Rendition* can help us to think about the relations and connections between various spaces that make up these distinctive cartographies of detention and torture (or, in the words of Derek Gregory (2006) the 'carceral archipelago' and the 'global war prison'). Furthermore, what *Rendition*, and other recent US films that broadly take the 'War on Terror' as their subject matter (for example *The Kingdom* and *Lions for Lambs* (2007)) are also able to do is to create visual connections between the carceral archipelago 'out there', and the everyday domestic and political spaces 'within' the West. There are, then, political possibilities within these kinds of films that can work to help dismantle binaries between the domestic and international affairs, and the indifference of Western policies towards actions being taken in their name. However, if these films chart and trace complex and ambiguous cartographies of violence and power, then as they do so they also produce their own complex and ambiguous politics, as we discuss further below.

Whilst the state of exception is, both visible and hidden, it is also highly regulated and yet, at critical moments, unrestrained. In *Rendition*, the exceptional is used as a form of displacement – a form of outsourcing and indicative of a new international division of counter-terror labour. While torture is shown to be ineffective, the film does not really question the practice of rendition more generally. In *The Siege* the state of exception provides an opportunity for restoration of constitutional values and practices after a senior army officer kills a terrorist suspect. In *Iron Man*, the state of exception proves to be redemptive for an industrialist at the heart of the military-industrial complex and for the US military more generally. The superhero is able to use his exceptional powers, and lack of state-sanctioned oversight, in order to try and protect vulnerable Afghan communities.

Whilst each of the three films discussed are useful in highlighting certain aspects of the state of exception, there nevertheless remains some striking continuities between them. Each highlights the role of 'highly placed' individuals in determining the prevailing legal and political norms that will operate in, for example, the airport, the city and the 'black site'. In both *Rendition* and *The Siege* this role is taken by a number of individuals working in the higher echelons of the 'security state', whereas in *Iron Man* it is the eponymous hero himself who largely fulfils this role (though exceptional powers are deployed by others within the film too). In a sense, all of these characters are manifestations of a political desire to 'get the job done', without the need to play by the rules or to defer to the authority of anyone or anything else (including the law). In this regard, such films can be thought of as a cinematic rendering of a geopolitical desire to operate outside of established norms and the rule of law. Such renderings are a familiar element within the action-adventure movie. The Bond franchise is but one example, and the superhero movie is perhaps just the extreme end of such geopolitical fantasies and desires. Such movies can act as moments of political catharsis given that, for the most part, geopolitical interventions in the 'real' world are subject to a whole series of constraints and complexities (see Ó Tuathail 2005, for example, on intervention in Bosnia and *Behind Enemy Lines* (2001)). In this sense, the exceptional powers that Western security states have awarded themselves in the years

Discussing the practice of 'extraordinary rendition' whilst framed by the symbolic spaces of American democracy in Washington DC

since 2001, and subsequently depicted in film, are a realisation of long-held desires.

Films such as *Rendition* and *Iron Man* also rely on the familiar cinematic trope of *redemption*. In both instances, key protagonists come to realise the consequences of their actions and resolve to 'make things better'. Such attempts are of course, on one level, entirely laudable, and indeed, in the case of *Rendition*, one could read the entire tone of the film as 'anti-war' and as seeking to reclaim a democratic, accountable America from the clutches of the neo-conservatives. But as the analysis of Rachel Walsh (2011) shows us (in relation to both *24* and *Rendition*), there are some complex and ambiguous cultural politics at work in these kinds of movies:

> *Rendition* does not provide viewers with an education in the US's global war crimes and enduring regimes of surveillance; rather, it offers a (sentimental) education in how to emotionally reattach themselves, through the white maternal body of Isabella and Freeman's civic education, to the nation from which they have been increasingly estranged. (2011: 163)

In other words, it allows the audience, through the well-meaning, white protagonists through which the narrative is largely told, to glimpse a different America – one redeemed from the wrongs associated with rendition.

Issues of race and racial profiling are central to these practices of rendition, as indeed they are to the full range of exceptional powers utilised by the Western security apparatus today. It is the non-white body that becomes marked out as a potential threat. Conversely, in Western cinema it is very often white bodies that play the role of the redeemer. Perhaps a notable exception amongst post-9/11 films in this regard is the semi-documentary *Road to Guantánamo* (2006), directed by Michael Winterbottom and Mat Whitecross. The film re-tells the true story of the so-called 'Tipton Four' – four young British-Asian men who were arrested in Afghanistan in late 2001, shortly after the US-led invasion. Following their imprisonment and torture in Afghanistan, the four were later flown to Guantánamo Bay where they were held for over two years before their eventual release, without charge. Guantánamo Bay is perhaps the most iconic manifestation of the state of exception. As Claudio Minca suggests 'Guantánamo's space of exception thus becomes a powerful metaphor for the constitution of a new geographical imagination within which, beyond and despite all international laws and institutions, the arbitrary play between the suspension and exercise of the norm becomes *a taken-for-granted part of the functioning of global politics*' (2005: 410; emphasis in original).

Whilst such spaces and practices of exceptionality can never be reduced to the politics of representation, there are some significant ways in which visual culture helps to shape the wider cultural landscape into which such practices are defended, contested and resisted. Visual cultures can, for example, help to shape certain kinds of normalising discourses around an issue like torture – the TV series *24* is often cited as an example in this regard. Of greater concern to us here, however, is the ways in which, as stated above by Minca, spaces of exception become folded into new geographical imaginations. Such geographical imaginations can be thought of as composed of two particular elements – people and places. Thus cinema can help shape new 'imaginative maps' of security/danger, or of threats and safety, providing imaginative resources for audiences in a rapidly changing world. And, moreover, cinema helps to shape a sense of *differentially grievable lives*. This is a point forcibly made in the recent work of Judith Butler; that the excesses of the contemporary Western security apparatus are possible because certain lives are seen as expendable, as *not grievable*. It is under such circumstances that it becomes possible to reduce human life to the 'bare life' articulated by Agamben. For Butler, the visual and discursive framing of the violence visited upon others in the course of the 'War on Terror' is crucial to the shaping of (non-)grievable life. Moreover, such framings matter politically; 'the differential distribution of grievability across populations has implications for why and when we feel politically consequential affective dispositions such as horror, guilt, righteous sadism, loss and indifference' (2010: 24).

Such differential grievability is central to the workings of many of the films discussed in this book. Indeed, it is through the construction of particular affective registers and emotional affinities, via well-crafted cinematic techniques, that audiences are able to connect with certain characters on screen – but nearly always at the expense of other characters. Thus in *Iron Man* we are led to become involved in the journey to redemption of Tony Stark, rather than in the plight of the Afghani villagers that simply perform walk-on roles in the life of the eponymous hero. In *Rendition* we are similarly asked to empathise with the well-meaning liberalism of Isabella and Freeman, whilst recognition of the plight of Anwar becomes possible only when it is established that despite his place of birth, he is really 'one of us'.

The Road to Guantánamo, however, does perhaps work in a different register. For one thing, it provides little in the way of a sentimental act of redemption. As Bruce Bennett argues 'the film refrains from offering us a clear resolution, a closing down of the debates with which the film is intended to intervene, or a reassuring sense that their [the Tipton four] brutal treatment had had a positive or "redemptive" transformative effect on their lives' (2008: 119). Allied to this, the film offers a very different perspective. We do not see the brutality of the excesses of the state of exception through the eyes of well-meaning, liberal citizens of the West, but rather, as Bennett claims, 'we are shown events from a different angle of vision, that of marginal or excluded figures … the film constitutes a "reverse shot", returning the mediated gaze of the Western spectator' (2008: 112). It is this 'reverse shot' that makes *The Road to Guantánamo* so powerful, a power which films such as *Rendition*, however well meaning, ultimately lack.

4   DISTANT OTHERS

Following the pioneering work of the Palestinian-American scholar Edward Said (1978, 1994), it is now commonplace to claim that the non-Western world has been central to the articulation and reproduction of Western identities. Said's examination of 'Orientalism', that is British and French representations of the Middle East, remains hugely significant in shaping our understanding of how the West, especially those countries with substantial imperial portfolios, encountered 'others'. Specifically, Said contended that the Middle East and its inhabitants were routinely depicted as backward, mysterious and/or exotic while set against the modern, developed and progressive West. An entrenched hierarchy of places, people and practices figured within Oriental representations, especially in visual culture. The formal decolonisation of European empires did not offer any kind of cultural respite. As Derek Gregory (2004) has reminded us, we live in an era of the 'colonial present' and those oriental discourses and practices have endured and manifest themselves via US military engagement in Afghanistan and Iraq.

The notion of the other, moreover, is used in two senses; as a noun and as a verb with due emphasis given to the ways in which individuals and groups distinguish, identify, name and locate those outside a particular community and norm. Distance in this context might refer to both a geographical sense (with attendant ideas of proximity and remoteness) and a socio-cultural context, which highlights how it might be possible for a 'distant other' to live in close proximity. The presence of immigrants and refugees within host communities might be indicative of how others could be both socially distant and geographically close. The way in which 'other' places, people and cultures are represented in the media and popular culture is rarely unproblematic, however. In a detailed analysis of Hollywood's depiction of Arabs and the Middle East, Jack Shaheen (2001) has noted how the film industry consistently represents Arabs as mysterious, irrational, highly sexualised and anti-Western, with the most egregious including *Iron Eagle* (1986) and *True Lies* (1994). Echoing Said's broader critique concerning Orientalism within Western cultures, Shaheen also draws attention to why and how these representations matter in terms of shaping American understandings of Islam and the Middle East. This has arguably become more pronounced in the aftermath of 9/11 when Arab-Americans complained of harassment and demonisation. Organisations such as the Council for Arab-American Relations complained that Hollywood films, even those made prior to 9/11, such as *The Siege* and *Rules of Engagement* (2000), do not help because they perpetuate a view that Arabs are prone to violence and incapable of acting reasonably. In the case of *Rules of Engagement*, US servicemen are forced to open fire on an Arab crowd while defending the US Embassy in the Yemen. Footage of the ensuing massacre shows that the American Marines were apparently justified because even children in the crowd were shown to be shooting at the Americans. The inference seems clear – 'these people' are even prepared to put their children in harm's way and are taught from a young age to hate Americans. And it seems clear that film and visual culture more generally are credited with considerable capacity to shape prevailing understandings of people and places.

This chapter considers the manner in which the 'distant other' is represented and made to be 'distant', as well as the way in which the other speaks for him/herself, offering a critique and a parody of Western practices of distancing, othering and moral indifference. As before, this concern is explored through a series of interventions using some examples to illustrate different aspects of this concern. First, we consider the seeming indifference of the West towards conflict in the Balkans during the 1990s, through a discussion of *No Man's Land*. Second, we consider how the distant other provides an opportunity for America and the West more generally to show its superior military-technological capacities while saving a feminised non-Western other. *Tears of the Sun* is used to animate this point. Third, we investigate how and with what consequences the distant other might resist subjugation and marginalisation. The Turkish film *Valley of the Wolves: Iraq* provides an interesting example of a film provoking considerable debate in Turkey for its depiction of US/Turkish relations. In the conclusion to the chapter we consider some of the ways in which such representations of the distant other come to figure prominently in debates relating to foreign policy. In particular, we are concerned with how the distant other is presented as a 'problem' to the West, and the ways in which cultural representations can shape the response to such 'problems', either through engendering a sense of indifference, or by providing a simplistic solution (often violent) to a complex issue. We draw on Gearoid Ó Tuathail's notion of an 'anti-geopolitical eye' as a potential way of reading film; 'an eye that disturbs and disrupts the hegemonic foreign policy gaze, a way of seeing that ... persistently transgresses, unravels and exceeds the frameworks scripting Bosnia [or elsewhere] in Western geopolitical discourse' (1996b: 173).

Indifference to the 'Distant Other'

An Academy Award-winner for Best Foreign Language Film, *No Man's Land* is set in the context of the Bosnian War between 1992 and 1995. The film uses a combination of tragedy, farce and comedy to expose the absurdity both of the conflict itself and the attendant discourses of Western military intervention. In his discussion of the geographical scripting of Bosnia, Ó Tuathail draws attention to the way in which the journalist Maggie O'Kane provides a way of seeing that 'records the fractured lives and broken bodies of the victims of the war, lives that fall between the lines of official governmental cartographies of the war' (1996a: 171; see also 1996b). While it goes about it in a very different way, *No Man's Land* can also be understood in terms of this effort to displace the neat geographies suggested by lines on a map. This sense of being out of place and of falling between the 'official cartographies' of conflicts dominates throughout, as much of the film takes place in an abandoned trench between Serbian and Bosnian lines, where two soldiers from opposing sides become trapped. There is no remote satellite system to get a global view, no view from above. Rather, the perspective offered in much of the film is that from the ground, from the trench, a view that is partial, situated and lacking in clarity. Indeed,

Literally and figuratively trapped in *No Man's Land*, whilst the world watches on

this sense of a lack of orientation is evident in the fact that the opening scene takes place in fog, with the very first lines uttered being: 'Fuck me if he knows where we are.'

In this context, the fact that the film does not provide a clear sense of the wider geopolitical conflict is appropriate because it is precisely the clear lines of this conflict that the film seeks to disrupt. That is not to suggest that the film does not situate itself within wider geographies and contexts. This is done in various ways, using humour and irony. The 'bouncing mines' (mines that when triggered bounce into the air before spraying thousands of ball bearings across a radius of fifty yards) that are laid by Serbian soldiers near the beginning of the film have 'made in the EU' written on the bottom. While reading a newspaper, a soldier on the Croatian lines exclaims, 'what a mess in Rwanda'. And at one point in the film we learn that all the United Nations Protection Force (UNPROFOR) officers in Bosnia are unavailable because they are attending a seminar about media relations in Geneva. More explicitly, the film addresses the wider context for the events through embedding a sequence of news footage about a third of the way through its length. Against the backdrop of actual news footage, a voiceover outlines the 'background to UN involvement in the conflict' (see Myers, Klak and Koehl 1995). The sequence begins with Radovan Karadzic telling the participants in peace talks in Geneva that 'you're pushing Bosnia-Herzegovina to follow the same path of horror and suffering as Slovenia and Croatia. You'll lead Bosnia into hell, and this may end up exterminating the Muslim people!' Then, against the backdrop of actual news footage, the voiceover continues as follows:

Radovan Karadzic didn't wait long to carry out his threat. Bosnian Serb and paramilitary forces, largely helped by the Yugoslav Army, furiously attacked Bosnian cities, which were defended only by armed Bosnian civilians and the rest of the police forces loyal to the Bosnian government... Today Bosnians are still denied the right to defend themselves by a UN-imposed weapons embargo although at this very moment war continues without any signs of pacification. The tragedy of the Bosnian nation continues, and the only help they've got now is 120g of humanitarian aid per day.

The voiceover accompanying this footage is clearly framed in terms of a critique of Western (non-)intervention. However, this is one of the central aims of the film – a critique of the moral contradictions of Western intervention, a rebuke to the seeming indifference of the West to its not-so-distant 'other'. The moral contradictions of intervention are neatly summarised through the frustrations of characters that feel themselves caught up in a situation that has no clear rules of intervention. In *No Man's Land* a number of UNPROFOR soldiers (nicknamed 'the smurfs' by Bosnian and Serbian soldiers) manning a checkpoint voice this concern and frustration in the following way:

- Why the fuck are we here?
- Good question.
- I reckon it's simple. To stop the locals killing each other.
- Except we can't use force or get into dangerous situations.

Frustrated by the refusal of his superiors to sanction intervention that will allow the evacuation of the soldiers from the trench, an UNPROFOR officer uses the only leverage he has – the threat of media exposure. He aligns himself with a journalist from 'Global News' who threatens to broadcast a story about the lack of action on the part of UNPROFOR. In this way the film acknowledges that in a contemporary context where popular media are crucial to the way in which conflict is managed and represented, such media have the potential to disrupt hegemonic scripts.

At one point the film presents the unfolding coverage by Global News of the events in the trench:

> – For those of you joining us now, we have breaking news from Bosnia, where a few men are caught in no man's land. Our correspondent Jane Livingstone is there. We're waiting to see which measure, if any, will be taken by UNPROFOR. Is there anything you would like to add Jane?
> – Yes Olivia. I would like to repeat the words I heard here only moments ago. Neutrality does not exist in the face of murder. Doing nothing to stop it is in fact choosing. It is not being neutral.

Through the voicing of such frustrations *No Man's Land* explicitly challenges the way in which UN intervention in Bosnia was framed by an ethics of moral abdication (see Ó Tuathail 1999). Ultimately however, the film refuses to follow this critique through with a morally redemptive ending. Thus, while some of the UNPROFOR soldiers, members of the media and those stuck in no man's land all voice a degree of frustration, this does not lead to successful action. This is, in part, because the head of UNPROFOR in Zagreb lacks any protocols for dealing with a situation in which both sides agree and want the same thing (i.e. the removal of the soldiers from between the lines, the presence of whom is only serving to complicate the clarity of the opposing lines). It is also, and more simply, because they lack the expertise to remove the Bosnian soldier from the mine that will kill him if he moves. Faced with this inadequacy, the commanding UNPROFOR officer orders his soldiers to leave the Bosnian soldier in the trench while also making it appear to the assembled media (through the use of a dummy) that this man has, in fact, been rescued. This is crucial because it signals the intention of the film to refuse to use the issue of intervention in order to reclaim a narrative of heroic, morally redemptive rescue. In *No Man's Land*, the message is that if the script of intervention does not fit with what the rules of engagement dictate, then intervention is not possible, regardless of the consequences. Avoiding any clear resolution, the film ends in a state of tension, with a view of the Bosnian soldier lying on the mine in the trench, presumably waiting to die, having been rendered morally invisible.

Saving the Distant Other

When George W. Bush took office in January 2001, there was an influx of neo-conservative ideas and practices relating to US power and influence around the world. Many of his key appointments were Vietnam-era political figures that witnessed first-hand the debacle of the early 1970s, and consequently, the first few months of his presidency were marked by a relative withdrawal from the international arena, an unwillingness to become involved in the messiness of other people's problems. By contrast, Bush's foreign policy after 9/11 was informed by a willingness to use military force in order to pursue values such as liberty and freedom around the world. Indeed, during the first years of his administration, films such as *Black Hawk Down* (2001) and *We Were Soldiers* (2002) tackled US interventions in Somalia and Vietnam respectively with, in both cases, emphasis given to American heroism and the actual experiences of combat (see Carter and McCormack 2006). In these films and others, such as *Behind Enemy Lines* (2001) which was based on the real-life experiences of a downed airman in Bosnia, the focus is on a small group of (male) soldiers and their 'testing' experiences in combat zones (see Ó Tuathail 2005).

The role of the distant other is critical here, both as adversary and as victim to be saved/rescued by American forces. American military action is, as a consequence, represented as defensive and proportionate to the scale of the dangers being encountered in distant and unpredictable places. One of the most striking examples of a film that valourises US soldiers and their violence on behalf of distant others is *Tears of the Sun*, starring Bruce Willis as a naval special forces commander (Lieutenant A. K. Waters) tasked with rescuing Dr Lena Kendricks (Monica Belluci), an American citizen trapped in war-torn Nigeria. Kendricks had been working as a doctor at a Catholic mission, along with a few other white European Christians. With the security situation deteriorating, a small group of US military personnel, under the command of Waters, are ordered to evacuate her from the mission in eastern Nigeria.

The opening scenes of the film are important in terms of the characterisation of place and the geopolitics of the country. Television news footage is reproduced, purporting to show a country gripped by violence. As the news report notes the country has '120 million people, 250 ethnic groups [and] a long history of ethnic enmity'. There are reports of rival factions committing extra-judicial killings, children brutalised and civilians terrorised. The Nigerian state no longer seems to enjoy effective sovereignty – a 'failed state' in the geopolitical parlance of the 1990s. It is divided, so the television report concludes, between the Muslim North (Fulani) and the

Christian South (Ibo). As a result of the conflict, the presidential family was murdered and a rebel general installed in power. The religious/ethnic geography of the country is critical to the subsequent narrative and the moral positioning of the US soldiers in terms of their mission.

Thereafter, the story concentrates on the attempts of this small group of American soldiers to extract the doctor and return her to the safety of an American aircraft carrier located 'somewhere off the coast of Africa'. As the commander explains the mission, a large map of Nigeria is projected on a screen, which is used to show the geographical remit of the mission. They are warned to expect a 'hostile reception'. Once they land, they struggle to persuade Kendricks to leave as Waters warns her: 'This jungle is filling up with rebel troops … they will kill everything that they see, including privileged white doctors.' Upon learning that the remit of the rescue mission does not include her patients, Kendricks refuses to leave. Waters makes radio contact with his superiors who re-iterate that their task does not include getting involved with the conflict; the soldiers have their mission and it does not involve the widespread rescue of black African adults and children (cf. *Hotel Rwanda* (2004)). Waters eventually tricks Kendricks into leaving the camp – the other Europeans, including a priest and two nuns, decide to stay. As the helicopters depart, Waters sees the rebel troops advance into the mission and begin to attack those left behind. We thus reach a crucial turning point in the movie; in the face of evidence of mass slaughter at the mission, Waters orders the helicopters to land and he, with some reluctance from his men, contradicts his orders and agrees to walk with the party to the comparative safety of the border with Cameroon. In his review of the film in the *New Yorker*, David Denby argues that this 'twist' in the narrative is important in the framing of the film as a 'fable of American military virtue … The Americans turn away from self-interest and do the right thing; the nation's military purpose is moral in the end' (2003).

Having made the decision to rescue not only Kendricks but also the Christian Nigerians from the hospital compound, Waters and the men under his command begin the task of leading the group to safety. Unbeknownst to the party, they are being tracked by a ruthless gang of Muslim Nigerian soldiers who are portrayed as determined to kill them all. The film does not dwell on why this party might be so murderous in intent but their 'Muslim' identity is implicitly portrayed as significant in terms of judging their likely (violent) behaviour. Waters' commanding officer warns, via the radio, that they are in effect on their own because 'Nigerian air space' is unsafe – an unlikely scenario given the presence of a hypermodern US aircraft carrier stationed off the West African coastline. After a series of encounters and near-escapes in the jungle, the American soldiers decide to enter a village in order to stop an ongoing massacre. Waters tells his men, 'We are already engaged' and they save other Christian Nigerians and prevent women from being further assaulted. After the violent encounter, Waters is shown standing in front of the burning village slowly taking in the horrors that confront him – the dead bodies, the burning village and the wounded and injured. Nigeria, in this film, is shown to be an anarchic space with difficult physical terrain – a literal and figurative 'jungle'.

The party is consistently shown to be vulnerable to the advancing rebel troops. Filmed as if they were 'swarming' over the landscape, they appear relentless in their progress. A furious firefight begins in the jungle and continues on the flood plains of a river close to the border. Deaths multiply as soldiers and civilians die. Waters helps to rescue his comrades. Injured and hopelessly outnumbered, the fleeing party is eventually saved by American air power; large bombs are dropped and the rebel troops are incinerated. The American-led party finally reaches the border but the Cameroonian guards appear unwilling to open the border gates. Waters' commanding officer lands in his helicopter and orders the gates to be opened in another example of extra-territorial authority. Waters and his team are evacuated along with Dr. Kendricks, while the Nigerian members of the party are left behind.

Tears of the Sun can be understood both as a fairly typical example of the action-adventure movie and as a cinematic reflection on the politics of military and humanitarian intervention. Set as it is in a supposedly 'ethnic' conflict in Africa, it perhaps bears most resemblance to the Rwandan crisis of the mid-1990s, in which the Western powers appeared both unable and unwilling to influence events. In this sense the film might well be inter-preted as a critique of the non-interventionist policies pursued by the West during that decade, not only in Rwanda but also in Bosnia. Indeed, some critics have argued that this was perhaps the main political argument of the film – Denby, for example suggested that 'the overall meaning of the movie is that Africa has dropped out of the American consciousness – that we are guilty of neglect in places like Rwanda, and that we must act to stop atrocities in the future' (2002). The politics of *Tears of the Sun* are, however, much more complicated than this.

As well as being understood as a comment and critique of the failure of Western powers to meaningfully intervene in the humanitarian crises of the 1990s, *Tears of the Sun* must also be read as a comment on the geopolitical context in which it was released – two years after the US-led invasion of Afghanistan, and more or less precisely at the moment in which the US led the invasion of Iraq. Understood within these contexts the film takes on a different set of meanings. As Tarak Barkawi (2004) rightly notes, the image of the West (and in particular the United States) as an enlightened and militarised liberator is an important element in contemporary representations of Western military action in the non-Western world. *Tears of the Sun* is emblematic of a wider popular cultural tradition in the West of representing the native population as savage, irrational and hell-bent on using violence to settle matters – which in the case of other films, such as *Spy Game* (2001), is shown to be susceptible to manipulation by American intelligence agents in places like Lebanon while at the same time being able to manipulate well-meaning but politically innocent Western women. This is aided and abetted by public dialogues and discourses from the 1990s onwards about the dangers posed by failed states and wild zones in the 'Global South' where the authority of states was compromised. By way of contrast, the US soldiers in this film are shown to be capable of dialogue, to act with reason, and to resort to force only in desperate circumstances. *Tears of the Sun* mobilises colonial and humanitarian rationales for Western military intervention – feminised black men and women must be saved from the violent behaviour of other hyper-masculine and violent black men in particular.

As Cynthia Weber (2005) has noted, with reference to the rather more nuanced film *Safar e Ghandehar* (*Kandahar*, 2001), this kind of humanitarian narrative visualises a particular moral and spatial grammar of the War on Terror – needy, pitiful and feminised Global South subjects needing and willing to be rescued by Western saviours. These films help to re-map the geographies of international politics with the United States as a force for good willing to enter 'wild zones' in order to save non-Western others. In the case of *Tears of the Sun*, however, a white American citizen (and doctor) is a catalyst for the accidental rescue of those black African men and women. Without her presence, it is clear that this party of heavily-

'Tearfully grateful natives waving goodbye' (Barnes 2003); *Tears of the Sun*

armed American servicemen would not have entered war-torn Nigeria in the first place – those Christian Africans would have been left to the mercy of violent Muslim militias. Moreover, the military intervention depicted in the film is shown to work – and to be appreciated by those 'liberated' by the process. Jonathan Barnes concludes that 'playing as a paean to US post-9/11 interventionist foreign policy, *Tears of the Sun* is a film only Donald Rumsfeld could love... The film's concluding tableau seems a projection of the Bush administration's preferred finale to the Iraq adventure with tear-fully grateful natives waving goodbye as American helicopters depart, and a US-sympathetic government about to assume power' (2003).

The Distant Other Fights Back!

One of the most controversial films to emerge from Turkey in recent years is *Valley of the Wolves – Iraq*. Lerna Yanik (2009) has provided a compel-ling geopolitical analysis of the film and its reception in Turkey, noting that the film not only offers a positive representation of Turkey and what might be called *Pax Ottomana* but also conjures up a searing critique of the post-2003 American invasion and occupation of Iraq. The film provides a powerful resource for thinking about how it might be possible to visualise a certain generic form (the action-thriller) performing a rather different role in terms of projecting particular representations of place, identity and state power. So much so the film was accused of putting a strain on US/Turkish relations by its unflattering portrayals of American geopolitical power, at the same time as being lambasted for its anti-Semitism.

Valley of the Wolves – Iraq caused something of a sensation when it was released in Turkey – it was the most expensive, popular and arguably most controversial film ever released in Turkish cinema. The anti-American tone of the film mirrors a wider reaction against the US in Turkish popular culture at the time, which included a bestselling novel, *Metal Fırtına* (*Metal Storm*) by Orkun Uçar and Burak Turna, published a year earlier that projected Turkey and the US as adversaries. The film emerged from a popular television series about a Turkish secret agent and his friends who enter American-occupied Iraq to secure justice for some Turkish soldiers captured and humiliated by American military personnel. Therefore, the movie situates itself via a fictionalised depiction of a real-life incident in July 2003, when US troops arrested and hooded eleven members of the Turkish Special Forces who were operating in the northern Iraqi city of Sulaymaniyah.

The film opens with one of the Turkish men involved recounting the circumstances leading up to the hooding incident in his suicide letter:

> For all this time that we were in Iraq, we asked ourselves: what business did we have there? Over time we realised that those who conquered these lands always tormented the people on it. Only our ancestors did not do this. And, that day we did live up to legacy of our ancestors.

He then shoots himself while dressed in his army uniform. Thereafter, the story focuses on the efforts of a Turkish unit, led by Commander Polat Alemdar (Necati Sasmaz), to track down Sam Marshall (Billy Zane) and the other American soldiers responsible for the detention and hooding. Marshall is the living embodiment of the Bush administration's military strategy post-9/11. He is convinced about his mission in Iraq and resolute in using overwhelming force, *wherever* necessary – nowhere is out of bounds. He and his men are also culturally ignorant and geographically out of place. At the start of the film, they raid a wedding party and kill the groom and guests because they are convinced that the celebratory gunshot fire is evidence of 'terrorist' activity. In the midst of their assault on the wedding guests, a small child is shot in front of his parents because the boy sticks a branch up the barrel of one of the soldiers' guns. After that calamitous incident, the Americans then fire wildly, shooting the bridegroom, guests and children. Some of the guests kill a few American soldiers.

The survivors of the massacre are then shoved into an airtight container truck and sent to 'Abu Ghraib' prison. On route, in response to fears that they might suffocate, one of Marshall's men fires some bullet holes into the truck killing some of the prisoners in the process and then kills another American soldier who threatens to report the incident. While the survivors are bundled out of the truck, a Jewish doctor is shown packaging trans-plant-ready organs to the United States and Israel. The killing of civilians in Iraq by American soldiers is represented in the film as shockingly routine. The use of cargo containers and Abu Ghraib prison provide powerful visual reminders of how suspected illegal combatants were stripped, deprived of Geneva Convention protections and tortured. In one particularly shocking scene, the naked prisoners are forced to form a human pyramid by the soldiers with guard dogs in close proximity (no doubt with direct reference to the notorious Abu Ghraib photos; see Butler 2004).

Alemdar and his contingent attempt to detain and hood Marshall at a local hotel. At that stage, the group intends to simply humiliate Marshall and then get locally-based media to photograph and film the event itself. Having planted bombs in the basement of the hotel, the Turkish group are convinced that Marshall will not be able to escape his public humiliation. Unfortunately for them, the American commander uses some Iraqi children as a human shield and entertains them by playing the piano while one of his men defuses a bomb under his seat. Before escaping, Marshall cannot resist baiting the Turkish men about the state of their country:

> Look Turk … you love to brag, you have your own rules and you have
> unchanging Iraq policies and red lines. You always say no one can
> do anything here. Let me tell you something: we screwed up your
> Iraq policy and your red lines … How can you forget that you begged
> us to protect you from the communists? I will tell what drove you
> mad: we do not need you anymore.

The bride of the dead man, Leyla (Bergüzar Korel), killed at the wedding party becomes an important element of the narrative – revenge takes on added poignancy not just on behalf of the Turkish soldier but now in the name of those who were killed at the earlier Iraqi Arab wedding – all were, the narrative suggests, Muslims regardless of their nationality. While Leyla is persuaded not to become a suicide bomber by a local sheikh, she commits herself to helping Almedar and his colleagues capture and kill Marshall. Juxtaposing their image as occupiers, the American soldiers are also seen to be delivering aid and working in partnership with some Iraqi forces. While some may have benefitted from that aid, others are internally displaced as a consequence of the anti-occupation violence. And as the sheikh notes to Alemdar, the Americans 'gave the desert to the Arabs, mountains to the Kurds and kept oil for themselves and we do not have any place to go'. As the American soldiers encounter the Turkish forces, their shooting is shown to be indiscriminate and results in the death of so-called non-combatants. Marshall simply shoots someone for looking through a house window. The devastation is widespread, Almedar stabs Marshall with the aid of Leyla's family dagger after a desperate final confrontation.

Geopolitically the film depicts the American soldiers as brutal, ignorant and inept when it comes to dealing with local communities. Politically, the characterisation is fairly clear with three distinct groups being depicted as evil, corrupt and/or undesirable – the collaborating Kurds of northern Iraq, Christian Americans and most controversially, certainly within Israel and the United States, the role of an identifiably Jewish-American doctor shown to be harvesting body parts from injured civilian prisoners for transplantation to clients in Israel, the US and the UK. The Turkish special forces, like their American counterparts, are also ruthless as Alemdar and his colleagues kill three Iraqi Kurdish paramilitaries at a checkpoint within northern Iraq. However, the movie is also critically aware in the sense that some of the dialogue is in Kurdish and the narrative contains some acknowledgment of the Kurdish presence in Turkey, provided Kurds are not collaborating with the Americans or anti-Turkish elements.

While critics in Turkey and beyond were left rather underwhelmed and at times outraged by the movie's controversial depiction of characters and events, it is noteworthy not only for its explicit critique of US geopolitical strategy but also for challenging some of the dominant representations of Turkey as a loyal ally of the United States and the West and/or as an Oriental space with attendant anxieties and concerns for Western actors. The actions of the Turkish soldiers are explained, in large part, by the logic not only of revenge for the treatment of their colleagues but also a commitment to uphold national pride and honour. Released in the midst of strong anti-American sentiment within Turkey, the film coincided with widespread anger at the invasion of Iraq, the creation of a *de facto* Kurdish state in northern Iraq and Turkey's problematic relationship with the European Union.

The film not only tackles the use and abuse of American power in the Middle East but also considers multiple references to Turkish nationalism and the Ottoman Empire. In other words, the film is as much a critique of American geopolitics as it is a lament for the loss of a Turkish/Ottoman empire, which once extended over much of modern-day Iraq and the Levant. The Turkish soldiers in the film note ruefully the loss of empire and Iraqi Arab citizens are shown to be welcoming of their arrival in Iraq. Alemdar's desire to hood Marshall is in part motivated by revenge, but also informed by a willingness to reverse past and present Turkish humiliations. For the Americans, Turkey and Turks are considered disposable in the post-Cold War era, with the absence of the Soviet threat. *In the Valley of Wolves – Iraq* is suggestive of new possibilities for Turks to resurrect their influence and stature across the region.

Distance, Proximity and the 'Other'

Often constructed as a 'problem' within security discourses, the 'distant other' appears most prominently in such ways of thinking in connection with the issue of 'intervention'. The question of intervening in the affairs of another sovereign state is, in turn, one of the central issues within both the study and practice of international relations and, moreover, it is an issue that is increasingly couched in the language of humanitarianism and human rights (including 'right to protect'). Issues of how to relate to, or indeed how to understand 'distant others', therefore lie at the very heart of the practice of international relations. The three films discussed here address, in differing ways and with varying effects, both the lives of 'distant others' and this question of intervention. In the case of *Tears of the Sun*, we have argued that there is a tendency in this kind of genre to depict an idealised version of the West back on itself, or in other words to produce an account of Western intervention where the only problem lies in the mechanics of execution of the redemptive act by the heroic Western male. *Valley of the Wolves – Iraq*, however, works in an entirely different visual register. Here, many of the tropes of the Hollywood action-thriller, especially those that revolve around the US military's interventions overseas (for example, over-simplification, unsympathetic portrayal of the adversary), are reversed in order to *critique* the presence of the US military and the broader geopolitical strategies within which they operate. In this sense the film turns the discursive and rhetorical techniques of much American cinema and geopolitics *against* itself.

However, *No Man's Land* offers, in our opinion, the most thoughtful and ultimately rewarding set of reflections on the ambiguity and contradictions of the notion of intervention in general, and the West's self-image in particular. Offering a trenchant critique of the seeming indifference and impotence of 'the West' in the face of the Balkan wars, *No Man's Land* offers a cinematic version of what Gearoid Ó Tuathail has elsewhere termed 'the anti-geopolitical eye ... an eye that disturbs and disrupts' (1996b: 173). He uses this term to describe the journalism of Maggie O'Kane during the conflict in Bosnia, suggesting 'what O'Kane's anti-geopolitical eye does is release the dam and let Bosnia bleed into our world, on to our newspapers and on to our television screens. With the intense power of her prose, she corrodes the self-protective layers of indifference of the West' (1996b: 181).

It is not our intention here to review the extensive history of political, legal and moral debate on the issue of intervention, but a number of remarks are germane to our ensuing analysis. First, it is necessary to consider the geopolitical paradox that lies at the heart of these debates. This paradox can be summed up by Klaus Dodds' question, 'how can humanitarian intervention be justified when it occurs within an international political system premised on state sovereignty and norms of non-intervention?' (2005: 160). In other words, the practice of one state intervening in the affairs of another brings two international norms (the protection of human rights on the one hand, the protection of state sovereignty on the other) into direct conflict. Furthermore, far from being enduring 'universal truths', both of these norms are historically and socially produced, and thus subject to the play of language and the weight of discourse and debate. The formation of foreign policy, then, is necessarily a considered articulation of these competing norms, and thus the framings and discursive constructions brought to bear upon any given situation or context are of considerable significance – see, for example, David Campbell's *Writing Security* (1998). The US-led War on Terror provides ample evidence of just such discursive strategies as justifications for military interventions (see

also Dittmer 2012). Fred Halliday (2010), for example, explores the extensive new vocabulary developed during the conflict for this very purpose;
Cynthia Weber (2005) notes the appropriation of the film *Kandahar* by
George W. Bush as discursive legitimation for the military intervention in
Afghanistan; and Stuart Elden (2009) argues that the US administration re-
articulated the notion of internal sovereignty (in the case of Afghanistan)
as a set of obligations to be met (rather than a right to be asserted), and
that if neglected, this made foreign intervention permissible.

Second, it is necessary to recognise that the practice of so-called
'humanitarian intervention' has greatly increased in recent decades, and
thus a better understanding of its construction – politically, culturally
and morally – is an important project. A dramatic increase in the use of
'humanitarianism' as a guiding logic for military intervention took hold in
the early 1990s, in the immediate aftermath of the ending of the Cold War.
Thomas Weiss, for example, notes that the UN Security Council passed
twice as many resolutions between 1990 and 1994 than it had in the previous 45 years of its existence, and that that during the 1990s 'humanitarian
issues have played a historically unprecedented role in international politics' (2004: 136). As this chapter has shown, this upsurge in 'humanitarian
intervention', and the ethical and political questions it raises, has been
reflected in a wide array of films. Indeed, the argument has been made
elsewhere that cinema itself can be seen as a form of intervention into the
'logics' of intervention (see Carter and McCormack 2006).

Third, and finally, this upsurge in the incidence of 'intervention' does
need to be contextualised within the discursive and visual practices (of
which film is certainly part) that make it possible. Despite recent attempts
to codify the criteria under which intervention should happen (such as
the Responsibility to Protect protocols; see Bellamy 2008), decisions to
intervene essentially remain based upon firstly, some notion of 'Western
interest', and secondly, a series of discursive justifications. In other
words, intervention remains a case of 'selective engagement', and thus
an understanding of how such selections are both made and justified is
an important question. In this regard a number of scholars have proposed
the so-called 'CNN effect' – the idea that the foreign policy response of
Western governments to international events can be driven and shaped by
media coverage of those events. As the work of Jon Western (2002) on the
US intervention in Somalia shows, the reality is often more complex than

this, but nevertheless, the fact remains that the ways in which international events become framed and understood does play a part in international responses to them.

It is worth concluding this discussion with an illustration – that of the delayed, partial and fragmented Western intervention that occurred in Bosnia in the mid-1990s, and to which *No Man's Land* is clearly addressed. In a stinging critique of the 'failure of the West' to stop the bloodshed in Bosnia, Brendan Simms argues that the British diplomatic community hold a particular responsibility for such a failure. He argues that the British government developed a particular 'storyline' about the conflict in Bosnia that 'held sway for three long years of slaughter, siege and senseless brutality in Bosnia' (cited in Ó Tuathail 2004: 492). In other words, he argues that the British diplomatic community were able to articulate a set of ideas about the causes of the crisis and the likely outcomes of any Western intervention in the region that effectively made the case for non-intervention. Elsewhere, Ó Tuathail (1996b) suggests that there were two dominant 'scripts' pertaining to the popular representation of the war in Bosnia – one that understood events as a 'new Vietnam', a quagmire that would ensnare any intervening forces in a prolonged and messy conflict, and the other that scripted Bosnia as a site of a 'new holocaust' and into which the West must intervene in order to prevent the spread of ethnic cleansing. Whilst the former held sway amongst political and diplomatic elites (at least in the early years of the conflict), Ó Tuathail reminds us that there are other 'ways of seeing' (1996b: 173). Given the essentially discursive nature of political decisions over questions of intervention and questions of action on behalf of a 'distant other', this seems to us a potentially important role of critical cinema, such as *No Man's Land*.

5   HOMELAND

The word 'homeland' has become increasingly important in the post-9/11 political lexicon, often with xenophobic and racialised implications as well as gendered connotations that merge the private home with the national homeland. At the heart of the politicised discourses of homeland are a series of ideas concerning *who* belongs *where*; whether that refers to the 'place' of women in the familial home, the perceived threat of the Islamic 'other' in Western towns and cities, the role and status of migrant labourers in the advanced economies of the West, or the role of Western militaries in the homelands of others. In all of these cases, film (and popular culture more broadly) has the ability to either reinforce dominant notions of homeland, or to rupture and disturb the everyday discursive production of homeland logics.

As Amy Kaplan (2003, 2004) persuasively argues, the idea of homeland has emerged as a powerful addition to the lexicon of US national security debates, especially in the aftermath of 9/11. While not unique to the United States, the evocation of 'homeland security' is not without significance, especially as related to America's victimhood. Along with terms such as 'empire' used by both critics and supporters of the recent Bush administration, the term 'homeland' has been used not only to demarcate a particular geographical space (with definable borders) but also to conjure up a vision of a community unified with an agreed sense of purpose. In so doing, Kaplan and others have argued that 'if empire insists on a borderless world, where the United States can exercise its power without limits, the notion of homeland tried to shore up those boundaries. In the idea of America as the homeland we can then see the violence of belonging' (2004: 8). This sits uneasily not only with earlier American self-understandings that emphasised the mobility of settlers and the importance of immigration to the making of the country but also in supporting the unilateral intervention into the homeland of others.

Various forms of popular culture, including film, have shown that the term 'homeland' has a variety of connotations (perhaps most notably this has been shown in the recent US hit television series of that very name). While we have noted a geographical remit, it also conjures up a sense of native origins, birthright, common loyalties, claims to homogeneity, and a sense of rootedness and shared past (see Kaplan 2003). In the case of the United States, with its historical geography of extermination, immigration, expansion and mobility, this vision of the country as homeland has proven to be deeply problematic in recent and not so recent times. In the nineteenth century, this expansive sense of homeland had dire consequences for indigenous North American Indian communities and a variety of films such as *Dances with Wolves* (1990), *Thunderheart* (1992) and *Windtalkers* (2002) have attempted to tackle the historical and contemporary legacies (see, more generally, Shapiro 2007). Documentary films such as *American Outrage* (2008) are noteworthy for their attention to land rights disputes and the role of a federal government eager to protect the 'homeland' while undermining the rights of Native American citizens. Such cinematic interventions raise troubling issues about American national identity and the relationship that some residents might have with other places and origins. Would it be possible, in an era characterised by fear and anxiety relating to mass terrorism, to be of two places? For much of the recent Bush administration and now highlighted still further under President Obama, appeals to homeland security remain important in justifying increased surveillance and civil liberty violations as well as enhanced federal authority to monitor private and public life. The Edward Snowden affair has revealed the full extent of these contemporary surveillance practices – practices which have been something of a feature of a range of pre-9/11 films such as *THX-1138* (1971), *The Conversation* (1974), *Robocop* (1987) and *Enemy of the State* (1998), to name but a few. The invocation of 'home' (indeed its discursive construction) is an essential element in the official reasoning of the national security state and its elites.

Although, as Kaplan notes (2003: 10), homeland security might be pre-occupied with protecting the domestic population from external threats, in practice it may well be the 'home' that is transformed into a state of constant emergency (see *Olympus Has Fallen* (2012), for example), justifying further investment in security measures. Moreover, this state of affairs is by no means unique to the contemporary situation within the United States – there is, rather, a long history of such practices, in a range of geographical contexts. The German film, *The Lives of Others*, is an exemplar of this security-surveillance nexus and associated corrupting legacies. Differentiating internal and external threats and dangers becomes increasingly difficult as members of the East German Stasi seek to secure the 'dictatorship of the proletariat'. Does a playwright and/or stage director pose a menace to national security? In the contemporary context of the War on Terror, domestic citizens and residents have been accused of aiding and abetting 'foreign' threats (in the UK, the US and elsewhere), and damaging rumours circulated in the United States of some Arab-Americans and Muslim-Americans 'celebrating' the news that New York and Washington has been hit by a series of terrorist attacks.

In this chapter, therefore, we consider how films might help us consider ideas relating to notions of the homeland and belonging. This is achieved through three distinct interventions – the first tackles, with the help of a British film, *Dirty Pretty Things*, what it means to be an illegal resident in a homeland. Those judged in effect to be out of place contribute strongly to discourses of citizenship and belonging. Immigration officers, as demonstrated in this film, play an important role in policing the homeland. The second theme revolves around surveillance and a culture of fear in the homeland state. Thus, in the aforementioned *The Lives of Others*, we witness first-hand the consequences of homeland security for social and intellectual life in East Berlin in the latter years of the Cold War. As with other national security states, the German Democratic Republic (GDR) and its secret service, the Stasi, are intrinsically suspicious of intellectuals and artists with their willingness to comment on and critique the existing socio-political order. The third segment features the Lebanese film *Under the Bombs* and the struggle of a woman to find her sister and her son in the aftermath of the Israeli bombing of the Lebanon. It details evocatively and effectively the devastation caused by urbicide – the deliberate and systematic targeting of cities and associated infrastructure, such as bridges. The film's focus on the whereabouts of two people provides opportunities for broader reflections on what it means to talk about a 'homeland' that has witnessed countless wars since the 1970s and occupation by Israel and Syria. We finish the chapter by discussing the relation between 'home/homelands' and film in more general terms.

Homeland and Belonging

Although not animated by anxieties about terrorism and international security, *Dirty Pretty Things* offers a vivid portrayal of two individuals – a Nigerian doctor, Okwe (Chiwetel Ejiofor) and a Turkish woman, Senay (Audrey Tautou) living and working together in London. Located around the appropriately named Baltic Hotel, both work in the low-wage service economy. They are on the literal and figurative edges of the British nation-state and are illegal residents, forced to eke out a living close to the City of London. While Okwe is a taxi driver by day, he works at the hotel's reception at night. Early one morning, he stumbles across a human heart stuck inside a toilet in one of the hotel's guest rooms. One of the hotel's regular prostitutes provided him with a tip-off about a leaking toilet. As the narrative develops, it becomes clear that he has uncovered evidence of a transplantation economy, involving the illicit exchange of kidneys in particular by illegal immigrants eager to secure a fake passport and ID. Run by a Portuguese hotel manager, Juan (Sergi López), this trade serves as a catalyst for further reflection throughout the film on belonging, identity and the transplantation/exchange of body parts and sex. The Baltic Hotel, like the Baltic Exchange in the City of London, is a place of exchange, albeit weighted in favour of those with money and the right sort of 'papers'. Some people are quite literally disposable.

As illegal immigrants, Okwe and Senay negotiate the uncertainties of everyday life even if they appear to have fairly settled work routines in the low-wage sector economy. Fearing exposure and forced repatriation, they are forever having to exercise caution, which in turn leaves them vulnerable to blackmail and exploitation. Will their accents and embodied demeanours betray them as not belonging to the UK? Both live on a high state of alert and the sudden arrival of immigration officers at the shared flat not only causes panic but also vindicates their observant practices. On entering her flat, officers from the Immigration Enforcement Directorate tell her that neighbours have seen a man 'coming and going' in her flat. She is reminded that she is claiming asylum and thus cannot work for at least six months while her case is under review. Moreover, as one officer notes, 'lots of people are living in London with no papers at all'. Okwe is forced to flee the flat while Senay tries to hide any evidence of his illegal presence. Given their precarious existence, the occasional sharing of a meal between Okwe and Senay provides some respite and presents a rare opportunity to reminisce about other homelands and in particular their favourite foods.

The full horror of the transplantation economy reveals itself when Okwe encounters a Somali man in desperate need of medical treatment. While he performs some emergency remedial treatment, Juan is seen transporting truffles to another hotel manager. Claiming that he has the 'best truffles I have ever seen in England', Juan negotiates a price of $1,000 but rather than simply exchange foodstuffs, it is clear that he wants further information on Okwe. Juan discovers that Okwe trained as a doctor in Nigeria and explains later to him the nature of the transplantation economy – in addition to payment the donor receives a new European passport. While Okwe refuses to perform kidney removal operations, he has to endure the constant possibility that Juan will expose him to the authorities. Moreover, despite his obvious horror, Okwe would be deported if he reported to the police this clandestine trade. He does not have the option of being a 'good citizen' because this is not his homeland. He is not a 'citizen' of the United Kingdom.

Senay, on the other hand, has to find new employment because the immigration officers suspect she is illegally employed as a maid. She finds work at a sweatshop run by a British Asian man. After a raid by the same immigration officials looking for Senay, she is forced to perform oral sex on the boss. Her vulnerability is graphically exposed – as if the boss was saying to her 'if you want to belong then you will have to perform for me'. As he taunts her, 'Maybe I should call them … what can you give me?' He warns her that 'every night she will be raped in prison'. In a fit of desperation, she decides that maybe she should agree to donate her kidney in return for a new passport and hence an opportunity to cement her sense of belonging. On the second occasion the boss demands a sexual service, Senay bites his genitals and then flees the sweatshop. Haunted by the prospect of arrest and deportation back to Turkey, Senay abandons her flat and job in order to seek refuge with Okwe in a hospital morgue – a place where Okwe enjoys the company of his closest friend, a British-Chinese man, Guo Yi (Benedict Wong).

Distressed by her loss of employment and housing, Senay agrees to exchange her kidney for the promise of a new passport and identity. As an illegal immigrant and woman, her body (as she discovered at the sweatshop) and now her kidney appear to be the only form of collateral she possesses. Juan forces her to have sex with him (and as a consequence she loses her virginity) before he will facilitate the operation. Okwe, when he hears of her intention, volunteers to perform the removal himself so that he can ensure that it is carried out in a safe manner. He also demands that both of them should receive European Union passports and new identities. Unbeknown to Juan, Okwe drugs him and then harvests Juan's kidney, as it is clear that he has no intention of being part of the transplantation economy. On delivery of Juan's kidney to his contact, the latter asks why he has not seen Okwe and his friends before. As Okwe tells him, 'because we are the people you do not see … we are the ones who drive your cabs, we clean your rooms and suck your cocks'. With Juan incapacitated, they escape to the airport with the help of Guo Yi.

Notwithstanding their new European Union identities, they decide not to stay in London. Okwe returns to Nigeria to see his daughter and to deal with the consequences of being falsely accused of killing his wife. Senay fulfils a long-standing ambition to travel to New York and start a new life in America with the help of a cousin who is settled in the city. The film's ending is left deliberately ambivalent – they have clearly fallen in love with one another but will they ever be able to enjoy life together? While they have prevented their bodies from being subsumed within the transplantation economy, their identities have been transplanted. Senay, now as an Italian and hence European Union citizen, is able to travel to the United States and to enjoy greatly enhanced mobility as a consequence of her new passport.

Unable to settle as a Turkish Muslim in Britain, the film highlights a wider ambivalence about the political geographies of belonging in a Europe dominated by white Christians. Turkey is not a member of the European Union and Nigeria is an ex-colony of the British Empire. Although there are established Turkish and Nigerian expatriate communities in London, neither character appears able or willing (especially Senay) to gain any kind of advantage in terms of support networks. Okwe benefits more in the sense that he is hired as a taxi driver by a firm run by a British African citizen. *Dirty Pretty Things* thus offers some powerful insights into how the practices and discourses associated with homeland and belonging help to culturally and geographically differentiate people without papers.

Moreover, as a consequence of growing British and European anxieties about illegal immigration, the film asks us to consider what kinds of compromises and exchanges immigrants and those in exile make to a host community. Unable to work as a doctor, for example, Okwe is reduced to performing as a locum GP in the offices of the taxi firm's office. He steals drugs from a local hospital and in so doing curries favour with his boss. To refuse to treat the boss would be inherently risky. Senay has to perform oral sex on one boss and is effectively raped by another – the notion of consent here appears irrelevant. Who would she complain to? They are part of a vulnerable low-wage service economy underclass, working anti-social hours in the hotel trade and sweatshop industry. And if they had succumbed to the kidney transplantation economy, what would they have lost beyond a part of their body? As Okwe notes after he has treated a critically ill Somali man: 'They swapped their insides for passports.'

Defending the Homeland

The Lives of Others provides a timely reminder that the nexus of state-led surveillance, security and a state of constant emergency is not, and never has been, the prerogative of the post-9/11 United States. Set in the GDR in the mid-to-late 1980s, and written and directed by Florian Henckel von Donnersmarck, it focuses on the lives of writers, playwrights and actors living and working in East Berlin. Central to the unfolding drama is the surveillance-based relationship between an East German Stasi captain, Hauptmann Gerd Wiesler (Ulrich Mühe) and a playwright, Georg Dreyman (Sebastian Koch) and his partner Christa-Maria Sieland (Martina Gedeck). The Stasi was, as the film reminds us, composed of 100,000 employees and further enhanced by a network of informers – no one or nowhere was immune from the Stasi. The narrative begins in 1984 and the audience is reminded that 'glasnost is nowhere in sight … the population of the GDR is kept under strict control by the Stasi, the East German State Police'.

As an observation on the national security state, albeit one informed by democratic socialism, this film enables us to consider more fully the political and geographical consequences of surveillance and secrecy. As such it forms part of an established body of work within cinema – a body of work that includes, for example, *The Conversation*, *Enemy of the State* and a number of dystopian futuristic visions, such as *Fahrenheit 451* (1966), *Gattaca* (1997) and *Code 46* (2003), as well as films that explore the voyeuristic nature of film itself, most notably *Peeping Tom* (1960). Indeed, Catherine Zimmer has suggested that 'surveillance has been both a theme and practice of cinema from its origins and antecedents' (2011: 428). As the narrative develops, it becomes clear that two objects lie at the heart of the fundamental tension between those trying to protect the GDR from any subversive influences and others including a group of intellectuals with a playwright at the centre of the action seeking artistic and intellectual freedom of expression. For those charged with state security it is the tape recorder and the archive, while for their interlopers it is the literature in the form of journals and newspapers often with the imprimatur of West Germany – *Spiegel* and the *Frankfurter Allgemeine Zeitung* respectively. Wiesler, an expert in surveillance and interrogation, is seen initially teaching a class at the Stasi College on some of the skills needed 'to know everything'. He tells the class that 'the enemies of the state are arrogant ... it takes patience ... about forty hours work'. A student in the class questions his technique of 'non-stop interrogation' and asks if that is not incompatible with the stated ambitions of the GDR. He is told curtly that 'your subjects are enemies of socialism' and discreetly notes the name of the student who posed the question.

The opening scene sets the parameters of the unfolding drama – exceptional measures are justified in the defence of the GDR and 'socialism' more generally. After meeting his superior and old school friend, Colonel Grubitz (Ulrich Tukur), Wiesler is given a new mission on behalf of the state – he must carry out detailed surveillance on the playwright Dreyman who had earlier received state recognition for his work. While the decision does not surprise Wiesler who thinks he is 'suspicious', the Minister of Culture, Bruno Hempf (Thomas Thieme) has an alternative agenda – he will use the apparatus of the national security state and a prevailing culture of fear to coerce the playwright's partner, Sieland, into an unwanted sexual relationship. If she resists, it is made clear that her career as an actor will be terminated. In order to secure that 'relationship', he orders Wiesler via Grubitz to find incriminating evidence so that Dreyman's reputation can be tarnished. This is no hollow threat as Dreyman's friend (and favourite stage director) Albert Jerska (Volkmar Kleinert) had his career terminated as a consequence of accusations pertaining to anti-socialist/GDR behaviour.

Within days, Dreyman's flat is extensively bugged. A neighbour who witnesses the Stasi operation (conducted over twenty minutes of screen time) via her peep hole in the door is warned by Wiesler that her daughter will lose her place at university if she utters a word to anyone. Up in the attic of the building, Wiesler sets up his listening device and begins to record detailed reports of Dreyman's activities and conversations with others. Nothing escapes his attention, including sexual activity. He is a man of procedure who is clearly committed to upholding the ideal of the socialist GDR to the extent that he appears to have little or no social life. In comparison with Dreyman's flat, which is filled with books, journals and drafts of stage plays, the few glimpses we gain of Wiesler's flat reveals a man with few possessions and simple tastes. Unlike the loving relationship that clearly exists between Dreyman and Sieland, Wiesler relies on a visiting prostitute for occasional acts of intimacy.

Alongside the surveillance operation, the Stasi more generally perpetuates a culture of fear and obedience that extends to all areas of life. The distinction between public and private is irrelevant. Although there are undoubted 'gaps' within this state of affairs, citizens can never be sure when and where they will be evaluated and judged. No one is entirely safe from scrutiny and no one can be assured of anything, especially when it comes to how loyalty to the homeland is policed. On one occasion over lunch, Grubitz threatens a junior officer with punitive action for making a joke that appeared to belittle the president of the GDR. He is later demoted for his joke. It is this encounter plus the manner in which the Minister is sexually abusing Sieland that proves pivotal for Wiesler as an agent of the national security state. He begins to use his discretion – he edits his surveillance reports, he engineers encounters with both Sieland and Dreyman (or 'Lazlo' as he is known in his reports) so that, in different ways, they can begin to resist and even subvert the Minister's advances. Most memorably, he fails to pursue an encounter with a small boy in a lift in their shared building. The boy innocently asks Wiesler about his occupation and noted that his dad told him that the Stasi were 'bad men locking up people'. Wiesler just catches himself before asking for the name of the boy's father.

Wiesler's doubts about the true nature of the GDR coincide with growing evidence of contact between 'Lazlo' and West German authors and journalists. Notwithstanding the desire for total surveillance within the state, the presence of West Berlin and West Germany more generally is enticing for Dreyman and his artistic and intellectual friends. It is also a source of concern for those charged with monitoring this group. The suicide of his dear friend Jerska is pivotal for Dreyman. He begins to write an article about suicide (self-murder in the lexicon of the GDR) and discovers that no official statistics exist on the matter. Since 1977, they have not been deemed worthy of public record. For a state that is in essence archival, this is surprising. As Dreyman dryly notes, 'those grey men who ensure safety in our land and happiness' cannot bear to record something that should not happen in a socialist paradise. With the help of an editor attached to the West German magazine *Spiegel*, who smuggles a compact typewriter into East Berlin, Dreyman is able to edit his piece for publication. The importance of the covert typewriter becomes clear when we witness a Stasi expert comment knowledgably on the different models used by leading artists and intellectuals. Given the sensitive nature of this piece on suicide in the GDR, Dreyman tells Sieland that he is working on a fortieth anniversary play about the country. The editor tells him that his work will 'let all of Germany see the true face of the GDR'.

This political and geographical division of Cold War Germany is critical and haunts the final part of the film as Grubitz, under pressure from the minister, attempts to discover who was the author of the *Spiegel* piece. A GDR state-television report confirms that relations between the two Germanys are now under strain. The offending copy of *Spiegel* is visible on the desks of Grubitz and the furious Minister. All Grubitz can tell him is that an editor of the magazine crossed the border and spent four hours in the GDR. The Stasi lost trace of him once he crossed into East Berlin. Dreyman's flat is raided by the Stasi and they find nothing but 'Western literature' and 'Western books and newspapers'. It is only when Sieland is interrogated by Grubitz that they eventually learn that the offending typewriter is hidden in a secret part of the flat. Sieland, as so often in the GDR, has agreed to inform on her partner after being threatened with prison and the termination of her career.

The flat is raided but unbeknown to everyone Wiesler has extracted the typewriter in order to save Dreyman from exposure. Motivated as much by love for Sieland and disillusionment with the GDR regime, Dreyman is saved by Wiesler. Tragically, Sieland, consumed with guilt, is killed in a traffic accident; Wiesler is not 'reprieved'. Operation Lazlo has not procured results and he is demoted; his new role involves intercepting mail sent to GDR residents. A few years later, the collapse of the Berlin Wall and the intermingling of East and West German citizens at the border highlights how the German homeland has been recalibrated. For Dreyman, after an encounter with the Minister (now a businessman), he learns that he had been under surveillance, a fact that was clearly new to him. Unlike Harry Caul (Gene Hackman) in *The Conversation*, he is able to cathartically strip his flat of all the offending surveillance wires and listening devices. Moreover, he finds a stack of files in the Stasi headquarters, which in intimate detail record Operation Lazlo including the role of Sieland as informant.

The *dénouement* of the film is a touching one. Dreyman surveys Wiesler, albeit at a distance, and the latter is now delivering mail shot material to buildings in Berlin. He decides not to make contact. Two years later, on passing a bookshop, Wiesler notices a recently published book by Dreyman called *A Sonata for a Good Man*. On buying the book, Wiesler notices that the book is dedicated to him via his initials and Stasi identification code – 'HGW XX/7'. His downfall was caused by his willingness to care about the 'lives of others' but in doing so he earned the grateful thanks of at least one of his surveillance subjects.

The Lives of Others is a film that highlights one of the ways in which the notion of 'homeland' operates in the everyday lives of states and their citizens. In this case the primary register is one where the state mobilises a series of external threats to the homeland in order to introduce a series of surveillance measures against its own citizenry, supposedly for their own protection. It is an important film in this regard for a number of reasons, not least because it acts as a powerful intervention in contemporary debates about the rise of a new security apparatus in countries throughout the West that have historically been critical of such measures in one-party states, such as the GDR. It also very powerfully shows some of the ways in which 'homeland' has both a personal and political resonance, and that attempts at securing the homeland at the state level always involve consequences for the private lives of citizens.

But there is another sense too in which *The Lives of Others* makes an intervention into popular debates about 'homeland'. Thomas Lindenberger argues that the film 'is received outside of Germany as a generic film about totalitarian rule, which just happens to be set in an otherwise unimportant communist country' (2008: 564). For those viewers *in Germany*, however, this film, together with a number of other significant 'GDR films' (*Good Bye Lenin!* (2003), *Die Fetten Jahre sind Vorbei (The Edukators, 2004)*) as well as any number of novels and television programmes, forms part of a significant process of making sense of the post-war history of Germany, and of reconciling the 'two Germany's' into one new *homeland*. In this regard, Lindenberger considers the film to be a *West* German reading of life in the GDR, partly because the morally uplifting ending of the film (the act of kindness undertaken by Wiesler, the Stasi agent) has no basis in historical reality – that is to say there is no evidence of a single such case. Lindenberger argues, however, that such a plot device plays an important function in attempts to create a unified sense of homeland today:

> *The Lives of Others* offers such a fantasy in particular to the segment of German society that otherwise would probably not be able to generate an empathy and identification-based relationship to the East German past... It has to be read as a way to come to terms with the disturbing fact that 16 years after the democratic revolution, public life of the unified Germany is still and again haunted by the ghosts of this second German dictatorship, by the stubborn inaccessibility of the East German experience for West Germans, and by the divisive effects of a mutual understanding of the past. (2008: 563)

Imperilled Homeland

Under the Bombs is a poignant reminder of the searing impact of a country's destruction, especially its urban life and transport infrastructure. Directed by the Lebanese filmmaker Philippe Aractingi, the story revolves around a woman's search for her son who was staying with her sister in the south of Lebanon. The prevailing context is made clear right at the start of the film, as television pictures of the Israeli bombardment of the country show the fear and panic of residents as they face a hail of gunfire. As the film reminds us, in July 2006 Lebanon and its people endured 33 days of such military engagement while Hezbollah was launching rocket attacks on northern Israel. It is noted that over a thousand people died and one million became refugees. The film was released only a year after the Israeli barrage and the State of Israel is a haunting presence throughout – the country's name is broadcast on radio and television programmes and spoken and shouted by angry crowds in Lebanon.

After a long journey from Dubai via Turkey, the main character Zeina Nasrueddin (Nada Abou Farhat) arrives in Beirut seeking a taxi driver to take her to the south of the country. Right from the start of the movie, the geography of Lebanon is a perennial feature of the conversations between Zeina and others, including taxi drivers and foreign aid workers. Only one taxi driver, Tony (Georges Khabbaz), will take her south to Tyre, Saida and her village, Kherbet Selm. Having agreed a fare, the narrative is subsequently dominated by their southern journey and frequently fraught attempt to discover the whereabouts of her son and sister. As they pass through wrecked buildings and bridges, they are forced to navigate their way through Lebanon's fragmented infrastructure. News reports via the car radio merely confirm what Zeina can witness for herself via the car window. The country appears to be in ruins.

As they stop at various places where survivors might have gathered, she learns more about the atrocious experiences of those who endured the bombings. Families destroyed, abandoned and simply missing. As one woman notes bitterly: 'That's what Israel wants.' Despite her attempts to garner further information from those who know the villages and towns of Kherbet Selm, Saida, Tebnine and Rmeich, Zeina cannot discover the location of her missing son. She travels with Tony to a nun's refuge in Marjeyoun in the hope of finding out information and as they travel in the car Tony speaks of his dreams of travelling to Germany so that he can open a Lebanese restaurant with his family members already there. As they travel onwards, radio reports confirm further losses and destruction in other places such as Taibe and Adaisse. After no joy at the nunnery, they eventually find her sister's house in the village. It has been destroyed and eyewitnesses tell her that she was killed even though her son was saved by French journalists and may have been taken to Tyre. Her sister may have also been buried in a communal grave there.

As Tony attempts to gather more information about the incident, he bumps into a child who knew Zeina's son. The child tells him that they hid for over ten days in a basement and that Zeina's son survived. Tony and Zeina therefore travel to Tyre and visit a military barracks there in the hope of finding out more. While the international political backdrop to the film is unquestionably the Israeli bombardment of Lebanon, a Lebanese military commander picks up Tony's brother's involvement with the South Lebanese Army (SLA). Asking him where he is from (Qlaiaa), and noting his surname, the Commander in a subtle but knowing way highlights the bitterness and anger felt towards those who collaborated with the Israelis in southern Lebanon. (The SLA was supported by Israel between 1982–2000 in the hope that it would defeat both the Palestinian Liberation Organization and Hezbollah. Some of the SLA veterans received financial compensation from Israel when they withdrew from southern Lebanon while military courts in Lebanon tried other former members.) Tony's family connections are thus an important element in the film's discussion of not only the shattered nature of Lebanon but also the way in which the Lebanese homeland is riven with schisms – ethnic, religious and political. Tony believed that he was being denied a Lebanese passport because of his brother's past involvement with the SLA.

As crowds, composed predominantly of young men, gather to chant anti-Israel and anti-US slogans close to where Zeina thinks her sister is buried, she tells Tony: 'This was not my sister's war ... we have known nothing but war ... America, Israel, the Hezbollah, Syria or Iran – I don't care.' She recalls the devastation visited upon Lebanon – 1975, 1982, 1984, 1989, 1996 and 2006. The dates provide a simple but powerful reminder that this country has had to endure widespread fighting and devastation. And yet in other parts of the film, as they are driving and walking through fields and mountains, a pastoral vision of the country is offered, dominated by olive trees and farming.

The film seems to suggest that geopolitical machinations are predominantly urban-based and that in the rural parts of Lebanon life is slower, simpler and thus not entangled in international political connections and webs of destruction. But it also hints at a recurrent nostalgia for a pacific Lebanon. As the camera lingers it seems to implore us to ask – 'why do we have to destroy this country?' Geopolitically, however, the gesture is not innocent. A common refrain about Lebanon revolves around both its size and beauty and how it has been compromised by wider structural forces. This has led some to claim that a kind of 'paranoia' prevails that makes the Lebanese think that their small country will always be entangled in wars because of its unwitting strategic role for the whole world. One thing that has changed, say from the post-1975 civil wars, is the urban/rural divide. Although it is not dwelt upon, the 2006 war was characterised by the wanton destruction of Lebanese olive groves and fields by the Israeli Defence Force and the legacy of unexploded cluster bombs continues to prevent numerous Lebanese farmers from working their land since 2006.

As they travel further towards Tyre looking for international journalists, Zeina is forced to re-immerse herself in a world that she despises. Weaving between foreign and domestic journalists, speaking Arabic, English and French, she is able to negotiate and discuss with a range of people who might have information about her son. Frustrated by her apparent lack of progress, she notes bitterly to Tony that she only sent her son to Lebanon because her marriage was falling apart, as demonstrated by her husband's apparent disinterest in the fate of their son. Tony returns to his frustrations concerning his brother, the Israeli invasion and the conflicted nature of the south of Lebanon. Eventually, they discover that the missing son might be in a monastery, but it is too dark to travel any further given the ongoing uncertainties regarding this mountainous region.

They find hospitality at a house whose occupants are known to Tony. Over dinner, one of Tony's friends tells him that the Israelis call it 'death valley' and Hezbollah 'martyr's valley'. In their collective frustration, another notes: 'The south is not a land. It is a forlorn corner.' His friends are Lebanese Christian southerners and although not noted may well be former comrades from the SLA. Their house appears untouched by conflict and one rumour circulating at the time was that Christian houses in the south kept their lights on (in 2006 as in 1982) to ensure that Israeli jets did not bomb them. Unable to wait until morning, they travel by car along the precarious road towards the monastery. As further progress becomes impossible, they have to travel the final stages on foot. On finally reaching the monastery, they are introduced to a boy who knew Karim, but unfortunately for Zeina he confirms that her son 'stayed under the bombs'. Karim is dead.

As the film suggests, throughout their odyssey Tony and Zeina experience first-hand the geographies of conflict and collaboration with Israel and non-state actors such as Hezbollah. Zeina's travels act as a series of encounters with a homeland traumatised by conflict and dislocation. Both Tony and Zeina are constantly out of place as they meander through the devastated infrastructure of the country. As the film suggests, this is a country/homeland at the mercy of all kinds of unwanted interventions. And yet if there is a hope expressed in the film it is that of the people and the landscapes themselves. The kindness of strangers alongside that of friends combined with lingering shots of the Lebanese landscape empha-sises generosity and fertility respectively. Lebanon, with its complex geog-raphy, offers the possibility of providing a homeland for its inhabitants if only it was given the chance. The film is dedicated to the memory of those who fell under the bombs.

Imaginary Homelands

The notion of 'home' is central to the felt geographies of both fear and security. Within many anthropological accounts, for example, 'home' is recognised as a site of familial security, marked off from the dangers of the world 'out there'. Similarly, the idea of a national homeland often works in the same way – a safe national space in which citizens can feel safe and secure from the realities of an anarchic world. Such deployments of home as a supposedly safe space are frequent within cinematic representations of international conflict. This is perhaps most frequently depicted in those scenes in any number of war films, where soldiers in the combat zone talk wistfully of home, a home that is visualised as variously 'safe', 'feminised', 'familial', 'pastoral'; an idealised notion of home which is used to high-light everything that the war zone is not. Moreover, such evocations are fre-quently mobilised by the combatants as a means of explaining or justifying the military actions that they are engaged in; the horror taking place 'here' is necessary in order to maintain the tranquility of 'back there'.

Such juxtapositions are perhaps especially effective within film, as the narrative is able to cut between 'home' and the 'front'. Nevertheless, the consequences of the violence of the battlefield do of course impinge upon the supposed serenity of 'home'. This is nicely exemplified in *Saving Private Ryan* (1998), for example. Following the celebrated opening thirty minutes, a harrowing and visceral sequence depicting the D-Day landing at Omaha Beach, the film cuts to a typically pastoral scene of home; a mother working in the kitchen, gazing out of the window at a serene, peaceful rural landscape. As the camera lingers on this view, however, we become aware of a disturbance, in the approach of a military car along the long and winding track to the homestead. The mother instantly knows what this means – the death of a son, fighting the distant war. Typically within the war film genre, this is the extent of the intrusion of conflict into the home

The spaces of safety and domesticity are punctured by the effects of a distant conflict; *Saving Private Ryan*

and homeland – the grief of mothers and wives. The events of September 11th 2001 (and subsequent attacks in Madrid and London) have of course altered Western perspectives on the cartographies of security and danger that are implicit in the usual narratives of home and homeland, bringing violence itself into the apparent 'heart' of the homeland.

In some ways, however, as the films discussed above illustrate, such insecurities have long been a feature of other parts of the world. Recent events have simply exposed those in the West to the kinds of uncertainties and dangers that for much of the world have always been present, even in the spaces of home and homeland. The three films discussed in this chapter are good examples of this. We could, alternatively have discussed a number of US films that, in recent years, have articulated these new found concerns with regard to US homeland security, such as the heroic re-telling of the events of 9/11 in Oliver Stone's *World Trade Center* (2006). Whilst such films might be thought of as characterising a certain kind of myopia when it comes to the distribution of violence (focusing solely on the puncturing of US homeland security), such disruptions are presented in a far more thoughtful manner in *Three Kings* (1990) directed by David O. Russell. Set in the hours after the ending of the 1991 Gulf War, this is ostensibly a standard Hollywood action movie based around a predictable heist-driven plot (and thus bearing many similarities with the 1970 hit *Kelly's Heroes*) – under the leadership of Major Archie Gates (George Clooney), four American soldiers (the others are played by Mark Wahlberg, Ice Cube and Spike Jonze) set out to find some stolen gold bullion and inevitably run into trouble.

The moral complexity of 'military intervention' and the ambiguous geographies of 'the battlefront' and the 'homeland', are most vividly depicted in the interrogation scenes that run through the middle section of the film, during which Troy (Wahlberg) is interrogated at length by an Iraqi soldier. Thus immobilised, Troy is interrogated not so much in order that he will speak, but so that he will listen to his captor. His interrogator initially articulates his confusion with American culture by asking why one of its most important icons, Michael Jackson, sees it necessary to change the colour of his skin. At another point, his Iraqi interrogator asks Troy why the Americans are bombing his country. When Troy responds with the suggestion that such action is borne out of the necessity of maintaining regional stability, his interrogator pours crude oil down his throat. Perhaps the most eerily prescient scene of the interrogation sequence, and the most pertinent for the present discussion involves Troy being asked to imagine how he would feel if his family was bombed. The screen then cuts to a series of silent scenes in which Troy's wife, children and home are destroyed (we discover that precisely this has happened to his Iraqi interrogator in the course of the US military intervention). Here, the audience is asked not just to imagine what it would be like for the US to be bombed, but to recognise the equivalence of such events occurring in either Iraq or the US. Such a puncturing of the safety and security of the (US) homeland is presumably

Imagining the unimaginable: terror in the homeland, as Troy pictures the bombing of his own family; *Three Kings*

unimaginable to the audience – but of course such punctures are rather more commonplace in other homelands across the world as the Israeli film, *5 Broken Cameras* (2011) makes clear.

'Homeland' then, has taken on a new resonance in the years since 2001 – not least in its swift appropriation by the US government when establishing the 'Department of Homeland Security' in 2002. According to Cindi Katz, post-9/11 the US homeland has become a site of 'banal terrorism' – 'everyday, routinised, barely-noticed reminders of terror or the threat of an always already presence of terrorism in our midst' (2007: 350) She further argues that powerful, performative discourses swirl around the term 'homeland'; 'Banal terrorism produces xenophobic discourses around 'homeland' that work to narrow the channel of threat and danger. At the same time, its discourses produce themes of the nation as porous and perforated, but ready to be mobilised as a coherent agent against less coherent threats' (2007: 351). It is clear then that material and discursive practices around 'homeland' are both contested and of significant political import. What might, then, be the role or contribution of film in this regard? Film can either work to support the kinds of 'narrowing' discourses outlined above by Katz – drawing lines around the homeland and creating powerful discourses of inclusion/exclusion and of suspicion and guilt – or film can, albeit in complex and contradictory ways, begin to question some of our assumptions about 'homeland' – as we would argue the powerful scenes in *Three Kings* begin to do.

6   SPACE, VISION AND POWER

In this book, we have used a variety of films to help us think through how the spaces of international politics, whether at the border, within the homeland and/or in relation to distant others, is represented, embodied and experienced. If film has a power to represent and to move us, it is precisely because it can animate and narrate the spatial locations and encounters that make 'international politics' possible. As we have shown, our sense of international politics is not one restricted to the diplomatic and political worlds of government officials and their leaders. It is not one tied only to specific spaces such as government buildings and official meetings. Rather, it is to be found in a host of sites and settings, as well as relationships, taking in the home, the airport, the street, the border crossing , hidden and secretive spaces (e.g. *Zero Dark Thirty*, 2013) and other mundane spaces of everyday life.

In David Cronenberg's film, *Eastern Promises* (2007), for example, a shop, a house, a restaurant, a Turkish bath and a hospital provide the settings for a complex tale involving Russian and Turkish organised crime syndicates, an Anglo-Russian family and Eastern European prostitution. As the film progresses, it becomes ever clearer that the lives of the protagonists, some more vulnerable than others, will be shaped by international exchanges of trade, geopolitical flux (including the fall of the Soviet Union), and ultimately violence. While the ending of the Cold War was greeted with acclaim, and accompanied by hope of a better and more peaceful era of international politics, *Eastern Promises* articulates a vision that is darker and more sinister – there is plenty of evidence of ongoing enmity between Russians, Turks and Chechens. In London, at least, the post-Cold War era offered some Eastern European immigrants the possibility of travel, family life and business opportunities. But, as with *Dirty Pretty Things*, there is also plenty of evidence of a world still fundamentally structured by poverty, inequality and in some cases utter powerlessness – most pitifully, drugged Eastern European prostitutes.

We want, by way of a concluding statement, to formalise a way of approaching the relationship between film and international politics in two ways. First, we wish to give due attention to the agents, processes and sites through which international politics is 'performed' in cinema. Second, we turn our attention to a range of ways in which the cinema of international politics can be thought of as having a *materiality*. We conclude with some final thoughts on the relationships between space, vision and power and the cinema of international politics.

Agents, Processes and Sites

What the films and the themes considered in this book do is to help us understand the manner in which international politics is made and re-made in a series of places at a range of spatial scales from the local to the global. In our discussion of *The Terminal,* for example, we recounted how the plight of a traveller who found himself not only *de jure* stateless but also literally trapped in an American airport highlighted the complex and overlapping spaces of international politics. Agents of US sovereign power, in the form of the customs and border security official and manager, empowered by the federal government in Washington DC end up making a fateful judgement about a traveller who is the 'victim' of sudden geopolitical change, thousands of miles away in southeastern Europe. Through the persona of Viktor Navorski, *The Terminal* as a comedy/drama highlights the absurdity and perniciousness of an international political regime based on national sovereignty and the claims to citizenship and the sovereign ambiguities of the airport itself. Viktor's survival in the airport is shown to depend on his capacity for inventiveness and networking amongst a multi-cultural and geographically dispersed airport staff. Everyone he encounters in the airport is shown to have come from somewhere else and in some cases have settled in the US illegally. So Viktor's fate, in a very powerful and literal sense, was settled as much by bad luck and poor timing, as it was by the sovereign power of the United States to enforce global rules about travellers and the status of their passports.

So a film like *The Terminal* stands as a counterpoint to something running through other Hollywood films used in this book which represent and indeed celebrate strong male figures (in the main) addressing if not tackling the challenges and opportunities thrown up by international politics whether it be via diplomacy, trade, war and/or border crossings. In *Iron Man*, for example, an unlikely hero, the industrialist Tony Stark, forges his masculine identity and accompanying sense of purpose in the badlands of Afghanistan (see Dittmer 2011). Trapped in a cave, with a sympathetic and English-speaking Afghan doctor, Stark's creativity and opportunism is shown to be critical in facilitating his escape from captivity and subsequent mission to stop Stark Industries from supplying weapons of destruction to 'bad guys' in unstable parts of the world. Stark as an agent of geopolitics is fundamentally disruptive, as he imperils flows of weapons and money from interested parties in the United States and elsewhere including militia and terrorists based in Afghanistan.

Stark's path to redemption (as a responsible and globally-orientated citizen) is as much a personal one as it is one about America's place in the world. As with a host of other movies, whether it involves US cowboys, unlikely heroes (as in *Captain Phillips*, 2013), soldiers and/or policemen, international politics ultimately becomes equated with an American exceptionalism. In the case of *Iron Man*, America's belief in progress and civility is shown to be dependent on well-placed, rugged and talented men, assisted by loyal and domesticating women, prepared to support and defend America from its enemies, wherever their location. The film is a vehicle for rehearsing a contemporary form of American exceptionalism, albeit one shaped by a post-September 11th era (see Dittmer 2012). In the figure of Tony Stark, we have an appeal for a new kind of hero – one that is technologically savvy, and able to sympathise with the fate of others including vulnerable Afghan villagers betrayed by both rogue American businessmen and Afghan terrorists/villains. Unlike the hard bodies that Susan Jeffords (1994) identified as being emblematic of Reagan's America, epitomised by actors such as Bruce Willis and Arnold Schwarzenegger, Stark's rather more lithe body is defined by his capacity for creativity rather than destruction *per se* (and, moreover, is shown to be both damaged and artificially maintained).

So the manner in which films address this combination of agents, processes and sites is critical to the representation of international politics. But the combination of those three items is also profoundly gendered and racialised, as well as dependent on a host of other factors such as class, location, age and so on. Some agents have more capacities and capabilities than others. In *Dirty Pretty Things* the figure of the illegal immigrant, whether Nigerian or Turkish by origin, is shown to face, on a near daily basis, the palpable fear of being discovered and ejected from London. Their bodies are literally mobile borders, with even their internal organs caught up in a transplantation economy. Women are shown to face further insecurity, namely sexual exploitation, by opportunistic sweatshop employers and hotel staff members such as Juan. Through the lives of individuals and their stories, films such as *Dirty Pretty Things* are able to represent how international politics is part of the entangled everyday lives of British immigrants, immigration officers, African Men, Middle Eastern women and a host of other nationalities and ethnicities.

Scale is a critical component of the way in which international politics is assembled through a variety of sites. In our chapters on borders, exception, homeland and distant others, we have considered how individuals and communities are caught up and work with a range of scales, and how their trajectories come to stand for something more than the specific and the local. In a film such as *Tears of the Sun*, the fate of a group of US servicemen and the people they have been assigned to protect from danger in the jungles and marshes of Nigeria, is represented as indicative of a broader challenge facing the US. How does a country with extraordinary extra-territorial reach and military power respond to distant places, and how do these localised acts of humanitarian intervention contribute to a scaling-up of America's sense of purpose in the world? The lives of a few Nigerians and their Italian doctor become emblematic of a debate, global in scope, about the role of force (and the right to protect) in the current and future worlds of international politics. This is all the more poignant in the aftermath of a failure to intervene to protect Rwandan citizens in 1994, which culminated in mass slaughter.

Materialising International Politics

Social and political theory has recently witnessed something of a turn to materiality. The work of William Connolly (2002) is of particular interest here for, perhaps counter-intuitively, he foregrounds cinema in his materialist account of political theory. In doing so, however, he follows (if not directly) a line of thinking developed by Gilles Deleuze in his writings in cinema, especially *Cinema 2* (1989). Here Deleuze articulates an understanding of cinema in which he recognises the material and embodied ways that the 'time-images' of cinema work upon the viewer.

Embodiment is of interest to those concerned with cinema and international politics in two fundamental ways; first, the body on screen, and second, the body of the viewer. With regard to the former, the body as a site upon which political power is acted upon is perhaps most apparent in the chapter on 'exceptional spaces', and especially in the discussion of both *Rendition* and *The Road to Guantánamo*. Both these films, and others such as *The Siege*, depict the reduction of suspected terrorists to what Agamben has termed 'bare life' – a body without subjecthood. Once reduced in such a way, such bodies endure repeated torture and the accompanying denial of basic human rights. But the body is the site through which international politics is performed in a series of other ways too, as depicted in a number of the films that we have discussed in earlier chapters, whether that is the way in which the mobility of bodies is regulated through border crossings and checkpoints (*The Terminal, Divine Intervention*); the multiple forms in which the body becomes commodified in the illegal economies that exist on the margins of society (*Dirty Pretty Things*); or the ways in which race is repeatedly used as a bodily marker and signifier of 'threat' (*Rendition*).

Importantly though, film does not just *depict* bodies as sites of political contestation, but it also enrols the bodies of the audience into a geopolitics of affect (see Carter and McCormack 2006) – in other words, film has the ability to move audiences, to work on audiences in ways that go beyond the discursive and brain-centred processes. Thus, future accounts of film and international politics need to take seriously the ways in which cinema is able to make interventions into political debate through the circulation and generation of affective registers such as horror, fear, hope, pity and empathy. Filmmakers are, of course, adept at using filmic techniques (the use of the reverse shot might be one example and another might be the popularity of hand-held filming techniques used so effectively to convey terror in *United 93* (2006)) to try and produce such emotions and affectivities in the audience (as indeed are political actors – George W. Bush's

'Top Gun moment' is perhaps the best-known example, but it is by no means the exception). Recognising the co-constitutive nature of political performance from film to international relations, and back again is crucial in recognising the significance of the affective political register, but there are others too. Paying attention to the affective qualities of both film and politics helps us to understand how cinematic portrayals of geopolitical events, moments and logics *resonate* across different contexts. Thus a film like *Tears of the Sun* exceeds its representational logic (understood here as its specific setting – Nigeria, and the specific geopolitical issues that raises – should the US intervene in civil conflict in Africa?) and partakes in the construction of particular 'structures of feeling' within political entities that resonate across different contexts (how should the US respond when faced with 'evil'?; how best should the US protect 'the weak'?; what kinds of problems can US military force solve and not solve?). Such a film, then, when viewed by audiences in the context of the on-going War on Terror takes on political meanings beyond the specifics of its narrative setting. The production of certain kinds of shared emotions (horror, pity, empathy, anger) is a key part of the way such films work across contexts.

Vision, Space, Power

Throughout this book we have argued that film and international politics are related in any number of different ways. Films often take geopolitical events as their narrative/contextual inspiration; films can be used to help us understand specific events and issues; and sometimes films can spark an international crisis (recently, for example, the government of Kazakhstan complained about its portrayal in *Borat*; and protests were sparked around the Islamic world after a trailer for the anti-Muslim 'film' *Innocence of Muslims* appeared on YouTube). However, the relationship between film and international politics needs to be understood as more fundamental than one simply of film *reflecting* international politics. Rather, we have argued that the relationship is far more *performative*. Our particular perspective in this book has been to argue that international politics operates within and through a whole series of spatial imaginaries and formations – we have considered four in particular (borders, homeland, distant others, spaces of exception), but this is by no means an exhaustive list. We might have included others, such as the 'figure of the earth' for example. Further, our claim is that such spaces of international politics are envisioned and imagined through complex sets of representational and non-representational practices, including those associated with film and filmic cultures.

Vision, space and power thus work together in complex ways. Three main points serve as our conclusion. First, that any act or discussion with regard to 'international politics' is founded upon a particular 'vision of the world', what geographers often refer to as a 'geographical imagination' – an image held in the mind, for example, of the shape of the world, the locations of its threats and dangers, a visualisation of both its 'safe spaces' and 'wild zones', and a set of ideas about the kinds of people that inhabit those spaces. Second, that one facet of this 'geographical imagination' is to think of the world as having particular kinds of more or less permanent spatial structures – nation-states, for example, but also the formations that we have discussed throughout the book – borders, distant others, exceptional spaces and the homeland. Third, that the performativity of popular culture (in this instance film) is such that whilst these formations appear more or less permanent, and that this appearance of permanence and inevitability is in part produced through representational practices, the same representational practices can also open up spaces of critique that begin to question our assumptions about the world. Films such as those that we have discussed are implicated in the performativity of the international politics in complex and often contradictory ways, so that the task of critique is not just to decipher the 'politics of film' in regard to specific geopolitical settings, but also to think through the broader significance of film with regard to the very construction of 'the political world' in the first place.

FILMOGRAPHY

5 Broken Cameras (Emad Burnat, Guy Davidi, Palestine/Israel/France/
    Netherlands, 2011)
300 (Zack Snyder, USA, 2006)
300: Rise of an Empire (Noam Murro, USA, 2014)
A Wednesday (Neeraj Pandey, India, 2008)
Air Force One (Wolfgang Petersen, USA/Germany, 1997)
After Earth (M. Night Shyamalan, USA, 2013)
Al qods fee yom akha (*Rana's Wedding*) (Hany Abu-Assad, Palestine/
    Netherlands/United Arab Emirates, 2002)
American Outrage (Beth Gage, George Gage, USA, 2008)
The Avengers (Joss Whedon, USA, 2012)
Babel (Alejandro González Iñárritu, France/USA/Mexico, 2006)
The Battle of Algiers (Gillo Pontecorvo, Italy/Algeria, 1966)
Behind Enemy Lines (John Moore, USA, 2001)
Beit-Lehem (*Bethlehem*) (Yuval Adler, Israel, 2013)
Black Hawk Down (Ridley Scott, USA/UK, 2001)
The Blair Witch Project (Daniel Myrick & Eduardo Sanchez, USA, 1999)
Blow (Ted Demme, USA, 2001)
*Borat: Cultural Learnings of America for Make Benefit Glorious Nation of
    Kazakhstan* (Larry Charles, USA, 2006)
The Border (Tony Richardson, USA, 1982)
Border Incident (Anthony Mann, USA, 1949)
Border Run (Gabriela Tagliavini, USA, 2012)
Bowling for Columbine (Michael Moore, Canada/USA/Germany, 2002)

Canadian Bacon (Michael Moore, USA, 1995)
Captain America: The First Avenger (Joe Johnston, USA, 2011)
Captain Phillips (Paul Greengrass, USA, 2013)
Cloverfield (Matt Reeves, USA, 2008)
Collateral Damage (Andrew Davis, USA, 2002)
Code 46 (Michael Winterbottom, UK, 2003)
The Conversation (Francis Ford Coppola, USA, 1974)
Crossing Over (Wayne Kramer, USA, 2009)
Dances with Wolves (Kevin Costner, USA/UK, 1990)
The Dark Knight Rises (Christopher Nola, USA/UK, 2012)
Das Leben der Anderen (*The Lives of Others*) (Florian Henckel von
    Donnersmarck, Germany, 2006)
Die Fetten Jahre sind Vorbei (*The Edukators*) (Hans Weingartner,
    GermanyAustria, 2004)
Dirty Pretty Things (Stephen Frears, UK, 2002)
Dirty Wars (Rick Rowley, USA, 2013)
District 9 (Neill Blomkamp, USA, 2009)
Eastern Promises (David Cronenberg, USA/UK/Canada, 2007)
Elysium (Neill BlomKamp. USA, 2013)
Enemy of the State (Tony Scott, USA, 1998)
Fahrenheit 9/11 (Michael Moore, USA, 2004)
Fahrenheit 451 (François Truffaut, UK, 1966)
The Fantastic Four (Tim Story, USA, 2005)
Flashpoint (William Tannen, USA, 1984)
Frozen River (Courtney Hunt, USA, 2008)
Gattaca (Andrew Niccol, USA, 1997)
Goodbye Lenin! (Wolfgang Becker, Germany, 2003)
Harry Potter series (Chris Columbus, Alfonso Cuarón, Mike Newell, David
    Yates, UK/USA/Germany, 2001–11)
Hotel Rwanda (Terry George, UK/ USA/Italy/South Africa, 2004)
The Hurt Locker (Kathryn Bigelow, USA, 2008)
Jaws (Steven Spielberg, USA, 1975)
In the Loop (Armando Iannucci, UK, 2009)
Iron Eagle (Sidney Furie, USA/Israel/Canada, 1986)
Iron Man (Jon Favreau, USA, 2008)
Kelly's Heroes (Brian Hutton, Yugoslavia/USA, 1970)
The Kingdom (Peter Berg, USA/Germany, 2007)

Köshpendiler (*Nomad*) (Sergey Bodrov, Ivan Passer, France/Kazakhstan, 2005)

Kurtlar Vadisi – Irak (*Valley of the Wolves – Iraq*) (Serdar Akar, Sadullah Sentürk, Turkey, 2006)

Lions for Lambs (Robert Redford, USA, 2007)

The Long Kiss Goodnight (Renny Harlin, USA, 1996)

The Longest Day (Ken Annakin, Andrew Marton, Bernhard Wicki, Gerd Oswald, Zanuck, USA, 1962)

The *Lord of the Rings* Trilogy (Peter Jackson, USA/New Zealand, 2001, 2002, 2003)

Machssomim (*Checkpoint*) (Yoav Shamir, Israel 2003)

Mad Max Trilogy (George Miller, Australia, 1979, 1981, 1985)

Minority Report (Steven Spielberg, USA, 2002)

Mongol (Sergey Bodrov, Russia/Germany/Kazakhstan, 2007)

Monsters (Gareth Edwards, UK, 2010)

Nicija Zemlja (*No Man's Land*) (Danis Tanovic, Bosnia and Herzegovina/France/Slovenia/Italy/UK/Belgium, 2001)

No Country for Old Men (Ethan Coen & Joel Coen, USA, 2007)

Olympus Has Fallen (Antoine Fuqua, USA, 2013)

OSS 117: Le Caire, nid d'espions (*OSS 117: Cairo, Nest of Spies*) (Michel Hazanavicius, France, 2006)

Paradise Now (Hany Abu-Assad, Palestine/Germany/France/Netherlands/Israel, 2005)

Peeping Tom (Michael Powell, UK, 1960)

Rendition (Gavin Hood, USA, 2007)

The Road to Guantánamo (Mat Whitecross, Michael Winterbottom, UK, 2006)

The Road (John Hillcoat, USA, 2009)

Robocop (Paul Verhoeven, USA, 1987)

Roger and Me (Michael Moore, USA, 1989)

Rules of Engagement (William Friedkin, USA/Canada/UK/Germany, 2000)

Safar e Ghandehar (*Kandahar*) (Mohsen Makhmalbaf, Iran/France, 2001)

Saving Private Ryan (Steven Spielberg, USA, 1998)

The Searchers (John Ford, USA, 1956)

The Siege (Edward Zwick, USA, 1998)

Sous les Bombes (*Under the Bombs*) (Philippe Aractingi, Philip Aractingi, France/Lebanon/UK, 2007)

Spy Game (Tony Scott, Germany/USA/Japan/France, 2001)
Star Wars (George Lucas, USA, 1977)
Syriana (Stephen Gaghan, USA, 2005)
Taken (Pierre Morel, France/USA/UK, 2008)
Tears of the Sun (Antoine Fuqua, USA, 2003)
The Terminal (Steven Spielberg, USA, 2004)
Thirteen Days (Roger Donaldson, USA, 2000)
Three Kings (David O. Russell, USA/Australia, 1999)
Thunderheart (Michael Apted, USA, 1992)
THX-1138 (George Lucas, USA, 1971)
Top Gun (Tony Scott, USA, 1986)
Traffic (Steven Soderbergh, USA/Germany, 2000)
True Lies (James Cameron, USA, 1994)
United 93 (Paul Greengrass, France/UK/USA, 2006)
War of the Worlds (Steven Spielberg, USA, 2005)
Windtalkers (John Woo, USA, 2002)
We Were Soldiers (Randall Wallace, USA/Germany, 2002)
World Trade Center (Oliver Stone, USA, 2006)
Yadon ilaheyya (*Divine Intervention*) (Elia Suleiman, France/Morroco/
    Germany/Palestine, 2002)
Zero Dark Thirty (Kathryn Bieglow, USA, 2013)

SELECT BIBLIOGRAPHY

Agamben, Giorgio (1998) *Homo Sacer: Sovereign Power and Bare Life*. Stanford: Stanford University Press.

___ (2005) *State of Exception*. Stanford: Stanford University Press.

Agnew, John (1998) *Geopolitics: Re-visioning World Politics*. London: Routledge.

___ (2008) 'Borders on the mind: re-framing border thinking' *Ethics and Global Politics* 1, 4, 175–191.

Amoore, Louise (2006) 'Biometric borders: governing mobilities in the War on Terror', *Political Geography*, 25, 336–51.

___ (2007) 'Vigilant visualities: the watchful politics of the War on Terror' *Security Dialogue* 38, 215–232.

Barkawi, Tarak (2004) 'On the pedagogy of small wars', *International Affairs*, 80, 19–37.

Barnes, Jonathan (2003) 'Tears of the Sun', *Sight and Sound*, 13, 10, 66–7.

Bellamy, Alex (2008) 'The responsibility to protect and the problem of military intervention', *International Affairs*, 84, 615–39.

Bennett, Bruce (2008) 'Cinematic perspectives on the War on Terror: *The Road to Guantánamo* (2006) and activist cinema', *New Cinemas: Journal of Contemporary Film*, 6, 111–26.

Bialasiewicz, Luiza, David Campbell, Stuart Elden, Stephen Graham, Alex Jeffrey and Alison Williams (2007) 'Performing security: The imaginative geographies of current US strategy', *Political Geography*, 26, 4, 405–22.

Billig, Michael (1995) *Banal Nationalism*. London: Sage.

Bleiker, Roland (1997) 'Forget IR theory', *Alternatives*, 22, 57–85.

Bleiker, Roland and Emma Hutchinson (2008) 'Fear no more: emotions and world politics', *Review of International Studies*, 34, 115–35.

Boggs, Carl and Tom Pollard (2006) 'Hollywood and the Spectacle of Terrorism', *New Political Science*, 28, 335–51.

Butler, Judith (2004) *Precarious Lives*. London: Verso.

___ (2010) *Frames of War*. London: Verso.

Campbell, David (1998) *Writing Security*. Manchester: Manchester University Press.

___ (2003) 'Cultural governance and pictorial resistance: Reflections on the imaging of war', *Review of International Studies* 29, 1, 57–73.

Carter, Sean and Klaus Dodds (2011). 'Hollywood and the "War on Terror": Genre-geopolitics and "Jacksonianism" in *The Kingdom*', *Environment and Planning D: Society and Space*, 29, 98–113.

Carter, Sean and Derek McCormack (2006) 'Film, geopolitics and the affective logics of intervention', *Political Geography*, 25, 228–45.

Conley, Tom (2007) *Cartographic Cinema*. Minneapolis: University of Minnesota Press.

Connolly, William (2002) *Neuropolitics: Thinking, Culture, Speed*. Minneapolis: University of Minnesota Press.

Cooper, Marc (2001) 'Lights! Cameras! Attack!: Hollywood Enlists', *The Nation*, 10 December, 13–16.

Council of Europe (2006) *Alleged secret detentions and unlawful interstate transfers involving Council of Europe member states*. Strasbourg: Council of Europe.

Cresswell, Tim (2006) *On the Move*. London: Routledge.

Dalby, Simon (2008) 'Warrior geopolitics: *Gladiator*, *Black Hawk Down* and *The Kingdom of Heaven*', *Political Geography*, 27, 4, 439–55.

Danchev, Alex (2006) 'Accomplicity: Britain, Torture and Terror' *British Journal of Politics and International Relations* 8, 587–601.

Danchev, Alex (2009) *On Art and War and Terror*. Edinburgh: Edinburgh University Press.

Deleuze, Gilles (1989) *Cinema 2*. London: Continuum.

Denby, David (2003) 'Tears of the Sun', *The New Yorker*, 24 March.

Der Derian, James (2008) *Virtuous War*. London: Routledge.

Derrida, Jacques (1983) 'No Apocalypse, not now: Full speed ahead – seven missiles, seven missives', *Diacritics*, 14, 20–31.

Dittmer, Jason (2005) 'Captain America's Empire: Reflections on Identity, Popular Culture, and Post-9/11 Geopolitics', *Annals of the Association* of American Geographers, 95, 3, 626–43.

___ (2011) 'American exceptionalism, visual effects, and the post-9/11 cinematic superhero boom', Environment and Planning D: Society and Space, 29, 1, 114–30.

___ (2012) Captain America and the Nationalist Superhero: Metaphors, Narratives, and Geopolitics. Philadelphia, PA: Temple University Press.

Dodds, Klaus (2005) Global Geopolitics: A Critical Introduction. Harlow: Prentice Hall.

Elden, Stuart (2009) Terror and Territory. Minneapolis: University of Minnesota Press.

Gertz, Nurith and George Khleifi (2005) 'Palestinian road block movies', Geopolitics, 10, 316–34.

Gibson, William (1991) 'Redeeming Vietnam', Cultural Critique, 19, 179–201.

Graham, Stephen (ed.) (2004) Cities, War and Terrorism. Oxford: Blackwell.

Gregg, Robert (1998) International Relations on Film. Boulder, CO: Lynne Rienner.

Gregory, Derek (2004) The Colonial Present: Afghanistan, Palestine, Iraq. Oxford: Blackwell.

___ (2006) 'The black flag: Guantánamo Bay and the space of exception', Geografiska Annaler: Series B, Human Geography, 88, 405–27.

Gunn, Joshua (2008) 'Father Trouble: Staging Sovereignty in Spielberg's War of the Worlds' Critical Studies in Media Communication 25, 1–27.

Halliday, Fred (2010) Shocked and Awed: How the War on Terror and Jihad Have Changed the English Language. London: IB Tauris.

Herbert (2008) 'The politics of immigration', Urban Geography, 29, 1–3.

Higbee, Will and Song Hwee Lim (2010) 'Concepts of transnational cinema: towards a critical transnationalism in film studies', Transnational Cinemas, 1, 7–21.

Jeffords, Susan (1994) Hard Bodies. London: Routledge.

Kaplan, Amy (2003) 'Homeland security', Radical History Review, 85, 82–93.

___ (2004) 'Violent belongings and questions of empire', American Quarterly, 56, 1–18.

Kaplan, Robert (1994) 'Coming Anarchy' Atlantic Monthly 1 February

Katz, Cindi (2007) 'Banal Terrorism,' in, Derek Gregory and Allan Pred (eds.) *Violent Geographies: Fear, Terror and Political Violence* New York: Routledge.

Kearney, Michael (1991) 'Borders and Boundaries of State and Self at the End of Empire', *Journal of Historical Sociology*, 1, 52–74.

Levin, Thomas (2002) 'Rhetoric of the Temporal Index: Surveillant Narration and the Cinema of "Real Time"', in Thomas Levin, Ursula Frohne and Peter Weibel (eds) *CTRL Space: Rhetorics of Surveillance from Bentham to Big Brother*. Karlsruhe: Center for Art and Media, 578–93.

Light, Andrew (2001) *Reel Arguments*. Boulder, CO: Lynne Rienner.

Lindenberger, Thomas (2008) 'Stasiploitation: Why Not? The Scriptwriter's Historical Creativity in *The Lives of Others*', *German Studies Review*, 31, 557–66.

Mackinder, Halford (1904) 'The geographical pivot of history', *Geographical Journal*, 23, 421–37.

Mandel, Daniel (2001) 'Muslims on the Silver Screen', *Middle East Quarterly*, 7, 2, 19–30.

Mains, Susan (2004) 'Monumentally Caribbean: Borders, Bodies, and Redemptive City Spaces', *Small Axe*, 16, 179–98.

Mathiesen, Thomas (1987) 'The Eagle and the Sun: On panoptical systems and mass media in modern society.' in John Lowman, Robert J. Menzies and T. S. Palys (eds) *Transcarceration: Essays in the Sociology of Social Control*. Aldershot: Gower, 59–75.

McCrisken, Trevor and Andrew Pepper (2005) *American History and Hollywood Film*. London: Routledge.

Minca, Claudio (2005) 'The return of the Camp', *Progress in Human Geography*, 29, 405–12.

Myers, Gareth, Thomas Klak and Timothy Koehl (1995) 'The inscription of difference: news coverage of conflicts in Bosnia and Rwanda', *Political Geography*, 15, 21–46.

Newman, David and Anssi Paasi (1998) 'Fences and Neighbours in the post-modern world: Boundary narratives in political geography', *Progress in Human Geography*, 22, 186–207.

Ohmae, Kenneth (1999) *Borderless World*. New York: Harper Business.

Ó Tuathail, Gearoid (1996a) *Critical Geopolitics: The Politics of Writing Global Space*. London: Routledge.

___ (1996b) 'An anti-geopolitical eye: Maggie O'Kane in Bosnia 1992–93', *Gender, Place and Culture*, 3, 2, 171–85.

___ (1999) 'The postmodern geopolitical condition', *Annals of the Association of American Geographers*, 90, 166–99.

___ (2004) 'British acquiescence in the destruction of Bosnia'. *Geopolitics* 9, 2, 492–500.

___ (2005) 'The frustrations of geopolitics and the pleasures of war: *Behind Enemy Lines* and American geopolitical culture', *Geopolitics*, 1, 2, 356–77.

Ó Tuathail, Gearoid and Simon Dalby (1998) 'Introduction: rethinking geopolitics', in Gearoid Ó Tuathail and Simon Dalby (eds) *Rethinking Geopolitics*. London: Routledge.

Paglen, Trevor (2007) 'Unmarked planes and hidden geographies', *Vectors Journal*, 2, http://www.vectorsjournal.org/index.php?page=7and projectId=59.

___ (2009) *Blank Spots on the Map: The Dark Geography of the Pentagon's Secret World*. San Francisco: NAL Trade.

Power, Marcus (2007) 'Digitised virtuosity: video war games and post-9/11 cyberdeterrence', *Security Dialogue*, 38, 2, 271–88.

Puar, Jasbir (2006) *Terrorist Assemblages*. Durham, NC: Duke University Press.

Robb, David (2004) *Operation Hollywood*. New York: Prometheus Books.

Said, Edward (1978) *Orientalism*. London: Penguin.

___ (1994) *Culture and Imperialism*. London: Chatto and Windus.

Scott, James (1998) *Seeing like a State*. Stanford: Stanford University Press.

Shaheen, Jack (2001) *Reel Bad Arabs*. New York: Interlink.

Shapiro, Michael (1997) *Violent Cartographies*. Minneapolis: University of Minnesota Press.

___ (2007) 'The new violent cartography', *Security Dialogue*, 38, 291–313.

___ (2008) *Cinematic Geopolitics*. London: Routledge.

Sharp, Joanne (2000) *Condensing The Cold War*. Minneapolis, University of Minnesota Press.

Vaughan-Williams, Nick (2008) 'Borderwork beyond inside/outside? Frontex, the citizen-detective and the War on Terror', *Space and Polity*, 12, 1, 63–79.

Walsh, Rachel (2011) 'What stories we tell when we talk about torture: mapping the geopolitics of compassion and the post-Abu Ghraib national family in *24: Redemption* and *Rendition*', *Environment and Planning D:*

Society and Space, 29, 150–68.

Weber, Cynthia (2001) *International Relations Theory.* London, Routledge.

___(2005) 'Securitising the Unconscious: The Bush Doctrine of Preemption and *Minority Report*', *Geopolitics*, 10, 482–99.

___(2006) *Imagining America at War: Morality, Politics and Film.* London: Routledge.

Weiss, Thomas (2004) 'The Sunset of Humanitarian Intervention? The Responsibility to Protect in a Unipolar Era', *Security Dialogue*, 35, 135153.

Weizman, Eyal (2007) *Hollow Land.* London, Verso.

Weldes, Jutte (1999) *Cultures of Insecurity.* London: Routledge.

Western, Jon (2002) 'Sources of humanitarian intervention: beliefs, information and advocacy in the US decisions on Somalia and Bosnia', *International Security*, 26, 4, 112–42.

Woodward, Keith and John Paul Jones (2005) 'On the border with Deleuze and Guattari', in Henk Van Houtum, Olivier Kramsch and Wolfgang Zierhofer (eds) *B/ordering Space.* Aldershot: Ashgate, 235–48.

Wright, Lawrence (2007) *The Looming Tower.* London: Penguin.

Yanik, Lerna (2009) '*Valley of the Wolves—Iraq*: Anti-Geopolitics *Alla Turca*', *Middle Eastern Journal of Culture and Communication*, 2, 153–70.

Young, Damon (2007) '*300*: A Sparta for our times', *Meanjin*, 66, 174–8.

Zanger, Anat (2005) 'Blind Space: Roadblock Movies in the Contemporary Israeli Film', *Shofar: An Interdisciplinary Journal of Jewish Studies,* 24, 37–48.

Zimmer, Catherine (2011) 'Surveillance Cinema: Narrative between Technology and Politics', *Surveillance and Society*, 8, 427–40.

INDEX